ABROAD

An Expatriate's Diaries

Harriet Sohmers Zwerling

SPUYTEN DUYVIL
New York City

ISBN 978-0-923389-46-8

Library of Congress Cataloging-in-Publication Data

Zwerling, Harriet Sohmers.
  Abroad : an expatriate's diaries / Harriet Sohmers Zwerling.
     pages cm
  ISBN 978-0-923389-46-8
  1. Zwerling, Harriet Sohmers--Diaries. 2. Zwerling, Harriet
Sohmers--Friends and associates. 3. Authors, American-
-20th century--Biography. 4. Expatriate authors--Europe. 5.
Authors, American--Homes and haunts--Europe. I. Title.
  PS3626.W47Z46 2014
  813'.6--dc23
  [B]
                                    2013030116

I dedicate this book to all my loves . . .

IN SPRING OF 1950, I sailed on the ile-de-France to Le Havre with two hundred dollars in my pocket and no return ticket. I planned to spend four months in Paris, but after my first night in a modest but still-too-expensive Montparnasse hotel, I discovered a grungy place on the Right Bank inhabited mostly by foreigners where the rent was ten dollars a month! I moved in that very day.

Notebook One

The moon is full above the black satin Seine. The spring night gleams. I long to go out, to walk the short block to the river and descend the stone steps to the quay. The air smells of lilacs and sex. But how can I? Everyone tells me it is dangerous to go there at night, alone. I gaze into the tarnished mirror on the wall and am inspired. I'll disguise myself as a boy! Then I can sit on the quay and no one will bother me. I am six feet tall, thin, with an adolescent body. I stuff my long hair into a beret, put on my Brooks Brothers corduroy jacket and Levi's, and head down the narrow staircase, the grimy beige walls of which are smeared with unidentifiable substances, spots of blood, snot, cum.

Sitting cross-legged on the damp stone, I breathe in the dank odor of the river, gazing ecstatically at the oily, shimmering water and the conical roofs of the *Conciergerie,* opposite on the Left Bank. I light a *Gauloise Bleu* and breathe in the rich smoke.

Then I notice the man, who sits, like me, with his back against the wall. He too seems lost in contemplation, quietly smoking, unthreatening. But then he gets up. The tip of his cigarette is a glowing circle bobbing before him as he walks toward me. I stare straight ahead. He leans over me and says, in a low, insinuating voice, *"Bonsoir, ma petite dame."* I jump to my feet, scowling. I am taller than he. I glare down at him.

"Foutez-moi la paix! Fuck off!" I shout. But he only smiles oddly up at me. The disguise has failed. I climb the stairs to the street and walk back to my stuffy room defeated.

JUNE 20
PARIS

Back from Berlin, where I visited Nanna Marianne Benjamin. I am sitting on the terrace of the café Select, when an American I know arrives with a tall Swede, a painter named Sven Blomberg. Sven has large gray eyes, a long aristocratic nose, and surprisingly full, sensual lips. He is polite and intelligent. An erotic current flows instantly between us.

JULY 18
ERQUY, BRETAGNE

Sven and I have hitchhiked to Brittany. We sleep in a tiny tent, on a cliff above the sea. It is a cold night, with blowing rain and a hard wind. At some point before dawn, we awake, shivering. "Let's have some tea," says Sven. He puts *alcool* into the little cooking lamp, and soon the water is boiling. He pours it into the bowls. "Come," he says, and I climb over his prone body to get my tea, wearing only a long, heavy sweater. When I put my leg over his naked thighs, something happens. He's there, inside me! It hurts. I laugh. He laughs. *"Et voilà!"* he says. It's happened, and I actually bleed! After all my erotic experimenting, who would have thought I was still a virgin? He comes right away, and I roll off of him. We drink our tea.

"You know," he says, "I didn't really believe you when you said you were a virgin!"

"I didn't either," I say and we both laugh, with our arms wrapped tightly around each other.

JULY 30
ERQUY

A gray morning, calm sea, smell of pines, gulls crying. Last night my stomach was sick from too much wine. I roamed over the hills groaning and vomiting like a dog. There was a full moon, and I felt guilty defiling the clean, dry ground.

Later, same day. Just now, when I left Sven at the tent he commented, "You are not in love with me." It shocked me. Of course, it is true, but it sounded as if he were letting me know that *he* is not in love with *me.*

The sea is darker now. It will probably rain. Little girls are building something, darting among the rocks like tiny birds. Sven has done a beautiful small painting of the beach, with me sitting there this morning when I was recovering, a minute black figure. It is called *After Sickness.*

JULY 31
ERQUY

I am learning a good lesson here, how to live in nature, to not be afraid when storms rise and the wind sweeps over the hills, when the sun sets in the shaking ocean and that strange glow appears on the greens and yellows, like something burning. I will always be grateful to Sven for bringing me here, no matter what happens between us.

OCTOBER 2
PARIS

Walking home with Sven, I realize something is wrong. No! No more indecision, ambiguity! It hurts too much! I leave him on the pont Neuf with a brave speech. Turning the corner, I look back and see him leaning over the bridge wall like a seasick man.

I lie in bed in my little, cold, neglected room. Smoke a cigarette. Shivering, trying to sleep.

I suddenly realize that his Israeli girlfriend, with whom he has been living for three years, is coming back. It's over.

I sleep for two hours, dreaming that Sven has left me as I have done before, always to wake up in his arms. Not this time. I cry a little.

At 7:00 a.m. I sit bolt upright, dress, brush my teeth, and run downstairs to the quai du Louvre, walking like an automaton. In the soft light, I pass the sleepy old concierge, carrying a bucket. I take the elevator to the top floor. My key doesn't work, but the door is open. There he sits, on the edge of the bed in a blue flannel pajama top, with his thin legs, naked genitals, big black-rimmed eyes, a frightened look on his face. I shriek "I don't want it to end like this!" and dive onto the bed. He undresses me and holds me. He makes love to me and I weep, and then he weeps too. We lie back and talk.

How is it possible that he loves two women at once, or that he did but—it's my fault, he says— doesn't love me anymore? On and on, over and over, I decide, or realize, I love him. We take the bus to Montparnasse. He is weeping most now. It's all rather beautiful—two tall young foreigners saying good-bye to each other through tears . . .

All day, I feel dead. At night there is a Chinese dinner party with Buddy [Worth], Larry Rivers, Nell Blaine, and Nanna, [visiting from Munich]. The evening goes on and on, with American jazz records, too much food, wine, too much laughter. Nanna and I finally leave—sad, tired girls on a long metro ride. Two drunk men are in our car; one vomits and the other holds his head . . . a good friend that.

We go to the Mabillon café—drinking Pernod, singing the blues, walking home shivering. I lie in the dark in my icy bed. The sound of a step in the hall. A knock. "It's me."

OCTOBER 6, 1950
PARIS

She returns today. He assures me; he really believes; we will be together for a long time. Now, he must just make an ending. I am too exhausted to worry.

END OF OCTOBER

This strange winter begins. Cold, rosy light, early dark. Sven and I together in the tumbledown studio. We cook and eat and sleep. When night comes, we light the oil lamps, read, talk, make love. We light the coal stove; the clock ticks; the cat sleeps. This is my new life.

Sven owns a small stone house in the Basses-Alpes. It stands alone, among moody gray mountains, without electricity or plumbing. It is like a child lost in a vast forest. At night, when we light the lamps and put wood in the stove, the starry sky surrounds us like a giant bowl overturned above a trapped moth. To someone in the valley below, our flickering lights must look like fireflies in the dark.

Our little bedroom is up a chilly narrow stair; it shines warmly in the lamplight. We snuggle together under the old quilt, and I begin to feel his erection nudging my side.

Soon, we are howling with pleasure. Our cries float out into the mountains. Sometimes, I imagine that wolves and foxes hear us and howl back. It is the best time of the day, lying hand in hand under the heavy quilt in the rich black mountain night.

NOVEMBER 1950
BEL-AIR, BASSES-ALPES, FRANCE

Across the golden valley is Entrevennes, a town of thirty inhabitants, with a deserted château, and neither priest nor bakery. Now, I am alone in our house. It is *Wuthering Heights* weather—gusts of wind, blowing rain. From time to time a dog barks in the valley. We have only four small windows. Sven says the peasants make them like this because they get enough of the outdoors all day. Sounds true. City people like large windows. I just went out to shit under an almond tree. Some of them are full of nuts wrapped in velvety gray pads. There are bright green olives on the little silver trees. I hear dogs barking and the sound of a gun . . . rabbit hunter nearby. A rooster crows. I can hear the goats going somewhere; their bells tinkle like water over stones.

NOVEMBER 12
BEL-AIR

From Rilke's letters about convalescence (I am feeling mournful, as if ill):

> In the midst of the fields there are patches of dark land with ditches dug round them. They are empty, and yet they lie there as though the bright stalks roundabout were there for their sake, rows of bars for their protection. I asked what sort of condition these dark patches of land were in. They said: "*C'est de la terre en repos.*" So beautiful, you see, can repose be and so does it look beside work. Not at all disquieting, but giving you the feeling of a profound confidence and the anticipation of a great time to come.

Sven has just called me out to see a voluptuous pink cloud bank reddening the mountains. And somehow this little stone house is at the center of the compass, and we, in our small movements, are its fitful needles.

NOVEMBER 13

We are just back from a trip down the mountain to a village called Puimichel. It is almost deserted, more chickens than people. Now it is getting dark, and a storm is coming. The mountains are black, and the gray sky rests on their patient backs.

NOVEMBER 18

We sat all morning in the sun and read the Bible—some of the Old Testament and the gospel of St. Matthew. What a dangerous book it is! How it turns even us, who don't believe, a little fearful, a little solemn. It affects us like a ghost story for children, and even for us there is the sudden, inexplicable thought: maybe it's true! We are subdued, distant from each other. I miss the gaiety and wildness of my New York life.

NOVEMBER 28

Just back from Aix-en-Provence, where we slept in a studio with a view of Mt. St. Victoire, Cezanne's mountain. At the wedding party, an old Israeli from Paris recognized me and called me la plus belle fille de Montparnasse. When I told him I am Jewish he began playing Jewish songs and blues on his accordion. I got drunk and sang "St. James Infirmary," embarrassing Sven and the snobbish Brits at the party. A middle-aged lesbian, daughter of a famous general, sat on the floor with her head in my lap. A very rich woman, a Guinness heiress, said, Je suis pédéraste irlandaise.

Aix is a strange town, bourgeois and arty at the same time. Back at Bel-Air, I read in the papers about a tornado hitting New York—broken glass, schools closed, etc. Homesick.

NOVEMBER 30
BEL-AIR

It's a bright windy day— the mistral. I am feeling lonely and restless. I brood, get neurotic and hypochondriacal. Sven says, "Work!" He berates me for being "empty," dependent on externals. "You are acting like an adolescent!" He is ten years older than I. All I know is, I am not happy. Profoundly bored. I also feel guilty and superficial. Sven wants so much to believe that I am like him, a totally committed artist. But that isn't me.

DECEMBER 13

Snow is falling lightly and the dry leaves hiss at its touch. A dog howls in the valley.

DECEMBER 19

Snow. Sven and I throw snowballs. Ours are the only human tracks in the whiteness. But I find dog prints and the charming little emblems of rabbits all over the hill.

A magazine came today, with pictures of New York at Christmas. There is a lot of snow! I miss my city. What am I doing here in this medieval wilderness?

DECEMBER 28
PARIS

Snow, four hours of daylight, stoves.

December 31, New Year's Eve

Sven is ill. He lies with his face to the wall, fever-ish and infantile. I feel lost in a silent, empty world. War seems to be on its way. Fear is at the edge of my mind. Somewhere in this city they are dancing; music beating against the frosty windows, drinking champagne. And far away across the ocean, my loved ones, still in daylight, are thinking about the night to come. Will they be dancing too? How long this year has been!

Notebook Two

It's warmer today. A doctor is coming soon, although Sven seems a bit better. Our black cat sleeps at his feet. I would like to go out, but don't. I am being good and taking care of him.

Sven's ex-wife Mimi and her lover, Raymond [Mason] were here this afternoon. I don't like them but am being "civilized" and pleasant. I lent them my typewriter . . . what a mistake! It's like lending someone my lungs for a couple of days.

There is this oppressive, sickroom silence. Soon I will go to bed next to Sven in the hot damp sheets. How I wish I could go somewhere else, but I seem to have lost my old brutality, or maybe it's just that I have nowhere else to go.

January 15

Yesterday, we made a lovely trip to the *marché aux puces*. It was a rainy afternoon. A gypsy woman in a ragged fur coat and gold earrings wanted to read my palm. She had a rough voice—tight tan skin over sharp cheekbones. She grinned knowingly at me and called me "*cocotte.*"

In a small café in the middle of the market, a man was playing the accordion and beating a drum with his foot. Two girls danced together like mechanical dolls. They reminded me of the old Jean Gabin movies I used to watch at the Fifth Avenue Playhouse in the Village, dreaming of France.

Last night, our landlord, the chimney sweep M. Durafour, came to tea with us. He feels that the U.S. is to blame for everything that is wrong in the world. I complained to him about the police state atmosphere here, where one is constantly stopped and asked for ID.

I am really angry about governments and their paternal meddling in one's life. Being a foreigner makes it even worse.

Durafour is a Communist, a charming man with rugged looks and black fingernails.

Our cat sits on my lap in an erotic mood purring loudly. He looks up into my face with his beautiful, green-blue eyes half closed.

JANUARY 26

Earthly delights. Showers, singing, looking at myself naked, reading, sleeping, sex. Some days ago Sam [Wolfenstein] came over. There was the usual talk of politics, movies, literature, and behind it all, his crippled body, his helplessness, his grimacing mouth, trembling head, shivering nerves, loneliness. The night he was here, our cat had disappeared. He was gone all day, and Sven got angry at me for being so upset about it. I began to cry and he was furious. The next morning, as though weeping had worked, I heard that touching little cry at the door. There he was, back from some mysterious encounter. I worried all day that he might go away again. I feel an odd jealousy of his adventures.

JANUARY 31

Today was gray-green; dark at noon. In the afternoon, Timothy came over with Martin [Schmid], the shy young German with, as Tim says, the "gentle manner." Martin gave me a drawing, a nude. We spoke in French about art, politics, Germany, France. I gave him my Berlin article to read although he doesn't know English. Tim will translate for him, I am attracted to Martin—his shyness and his soft, childish mouth.

FEBRUARY 4

It is Sven's birthday. We went last night to the *Bal Nègre*. It was frustrating to dance with Sven and his old-maid English friend, John Scott, when I wanted

to dance with one of the black guys. I had one dance
with a short fellow who held me very tight. His sweating little face smiled slyly up at me as he pressed his
erection into my belly.

I wore my glass and silver earrings and looked
tender. The Arab lesbian I've never met was with
Michel, an old friend of Ann M., and sat on the balcony looking down wistfully at the dancers. Her
dark-ringed eyes were on me.

Mimi and Raymond are coming over tonight. Tomorrow we leave for London.

FEBRUARY 8
LONDON

Arrived last night in this wet, black city. We are in
a small, pink-and-white room, with one tall window overlooking a railroad yard and a smaller round
window framing immense, spider-like winter trees,
a yellow house with a shiny black roof, and two gray
steeples beyond. This morning it was filled with silver light bordered by the knobby black branches of
the trees. It has the quality of a painting, changeless and of another age. This is in elegant Regency
Square, close to Regents Park, framed by two-story
houses, white and pearly, with doors of different colors, often with black, wrought-iron balconies on the
second story.

FEBRUARY 10

Sven has gone to visit a friend in Oxford. I sit in the darkening room, feeling a little sad.

FEBRUARY 11, 1951

The zoo today in a wet yellow mist.

Things seen:

The birds of prey—vultures, eagles, hawks. The vultures; what we Americans call "buzzards" were truly frightful, with their long, bent legs, shoddy feathers, immense brutal wings, and horrible small heads on powerful necks. One tired-looking American eagle and a beautiful golden holding a piece of flesh in a giant claw.

A well-built brown gorilla performed like a circus strong man, darting bright eyes at me after each stunt. A man ridiculously mocked him. One silly-faced orangutan piled straw over himself like a child playing in the sand. A really ugly baboon with hairless pink breast, long hair like a cape over his shoulders, and red eyelids that turned white when he rolled his eyes, had a lurid red mouth and naked buttocks. He seemed jealous when a man played with a more approachable ape nearby and pressed against the bars of his cage making fearful faces. I felt sorry for him, so ugly, so alone, so fierce.

Three California seals played together and followed a passing guard hopefully, but he had nothing for them.

Lovely deer with bulging eyes like polished chestnuts.

Beautiful cats.

Went to the movies tonight and bought a threepenny piece of cake from a vendor with a Scottish accent, who gave it to me though I only had two and a half pence.

FEBRUARY 12

Sven phoned sweetly, saying he hadn't been able to sleep without me and is coming back tomorrow with forty-five pounds. Maybe we'll manage to get to Italy after all. I am still finding it hard to believe in this relationship. It seems so much more natural for me to be alone.

FEBRUARY 14

A night with the British poets in a new art center with big couches and a bar. Readings by unknown poets. The master of ceremonies was Herbert Read. He has a head like a gray pumpkin. He announced that Stephen Spender was present and asked him to read. Spender produced a poem based on interviews in Marx's *Das Kapital*.

The first one was a child speaking: "Heard say four times four is eight. Our King has all the gold and lives in a palace called London. Our King is a queen and his son is a princess. Heard say that God, who is a dog, made the world and all of us in it. Then there was a flood and everybody got drownded except for one man and he was a bird . . ."

Compared to this astonishing poetry, Spender's stuff was cold and banal.

Then there was an odd doctor with limericks and stories, a horrible sharp-faced fag with "traditional" poems about birds, and a handsome young Caribbean with beautiful, intense tributes to his island home. [Derek Walcott].

Emanuel Litvinov was next, with his Eliot-influenced poems. While he reads, Eliot himself enters the hall. Litvinov's face goes pale, but he proceeds to read a poem dedicated to him, an attack on his anti-Semitism. The audience is frozen in dismay.

There is bewildered applause and a very pregnant Jewish woman sitting behind us cheers loudly. Eliot looks coolly down his nose when a shrill voice cries out, "I am almost as Jewish as Mr. Litvinov and I protest this poem!" It is Spender, looking outraged.

Litvinov, with a horrible pale twitchy face, returns to his seat, past Eliot, grimacing foolishly. (I hate him for it).

Afterward, a "nice" older lady says to me, "It was in such bad taste! After all, what did Mr. Eliot have to do with those Jews dying . . . That's the sort of thing that breeds anti-Semitism, don't you think?" A very frightened lady, this. . . . The pregnant girl looks haughtily and accusingly at everyone, but she stays on. Her long dangling earrings tremble.

FEBRUARY 21

One star over the steeples in the circular window. Last night the electricity failed. We had three candles in the red candelabra and made love ecstatically to Palestrina on the radio.

Had a letter from Susan [Sontag] the other day. She has married a professor, much older than herself, someone "important." She says she loves me. "It is a transcendent fact." She comes to Europe in June.

MARCH 17
PARIS

How beautiful this city! A touch of spring the night we arrived. The April 1951 issue of *New Story* magazine is here with my first published story. My name is on the cover along with James Baldwin!

MARCH 20

M. Durafour, our landlord, talked to us all afternoon. I showed him my story and he asked what it was about. I said, *"Un homme et une femme."* He responded, *"Qui se rencontrent ou qui se séparent?"* It was a perfect question and shows what kind of mind he has.

MARCH 23

Sitting in the sun on the terrasse of the Select. I have been here a year. It is Easter again and the streets are filling up with wide-eyed young foreigners—Americans, English, German. How recently I was one of them, and now I feel like a Parisian . . .

MARCH 27

My birthday was a gray, quiet day. Sven made lovely gestures of celebration: an Easter egg, red and gold flowers, an especially nice cheese for breakfast. We went to St. Michel to see *Le jour se léve,* and sat for hours at the Royal and, later, the Dôme watching people pass. I am twenty-two.

Sven looked into these pages the other day, and now I am feeling a certain inhibition in writing about other people, for example, Martin. Still, I must have my privacy and freedom, even as he becomes more jealous all the time.

APRIL 5

Coming home in the metro, I saw a beautiful young nun, walking quickly, with slim, nervous hands twirling her rosary. I kept looking at her and she returned my look with knowing eyes. For some reason, I have always been attracted to nuns . . .

APRIL 19

I am reading the letters of Katherine Mansfield, with whom I easily identify. I have been compared to her often by English teachers like dear old Miss Wheeler in high school.

Yesterday, I reread Faulkner's *Sanctuary*. It is powerful and erotic although not as masterful as *The Sound and the Fury*.

APRIL 22

We took a train to Meudon—trees all blossoming, children carrying tiny banners and gathering the budding branches, strong sun.

When we came back to town, we walked through the Flea Market at Vanves. A man with a sad moustache in an old patched coat was selling needle threaders. He had a suitcase full of thread and a little white mouse he put into his pocket when the crowds moved away.

A group of laughing toddlers sitting on the step of a wine shop. One of the girls, about five, has her legs open wide so you can see her protruding pubis. An old woman comes out and, noticing , pulls her skirt down roughly.

Last night, I was waiting in the metro for Helen [de Mott] who is visiting. Two little girls stuck their tongues out at me, sassing me in an argot I don't understand. The bolder of the two sneaked up and stepped lightly on my foot.

Helen and I went to the Montagne Sainte-Geneviève, a lesbian bar. The tough young dykes attract me strangely. In a way, I would love to be like them, but I am definitely not.

I certainly am not "femme" either.

MAY 2
LONDON

The National Gallery . . . so rich!

May 6

Today at the Festival of Britain. It is beautiful—flags flying along the river, curtains of colored balls glowing against the city grime. There was a handsome white horse in the livestock exhibition. People were laughing and pointing at him. I have never understood such behavior. How can they be so sure that the animal does not feel their nasty attitude? I always sense their intelligence and awareness. I could no more laugh at a horse than at a child.

May 26
Forio d'Ischia, Italy

We live on the edge of a quiet little sea. It is not yet nine in the morning, but we have been up for hours. Sven is sitting in our large, high room with its stone floor, low bed, and its jars and cans of flowers—yellow and white daisies, long-stemmed red sweet peas and in a green glass, one fat, pink rose.

The town is to our left in the curve of the bay. It has an ancient, bleached, almost African look. The houses are white or pink or a tawny old yellow. There are occasional little cupolas and red and black striped house fronts. A few small boats sit on the beach, and nearby, on a stone breakwater, is a lopsided white church. Its bell tolls over the water, in a strange, shaken rhythm.

Two boys pass with a skinny little dog on a knotted rope. When he slows or stops they hit him with a bamboo stick. One of the boys is singing sweetly. Poor little dog; are they going to drown it?

Ten minutes later they return, without the dog. They laugh and sing. Brutal with animals, the Italians!

JUNE 3
FORIO

We went to Capri this week and stayed with Martha [Strater] and her Swedish girlfriend, a plump young blonde with a cat-like face, who admires Rimbaud. I danced in the nightclub with a phony Italian gigolo and with Sven, who is self-conscious and stiff. I wanted to dance with Martha but the atmosphere did not encourage it.

Later, Sven and I had a terrible argument about my "lesbian" behavior. I was so tired I didn't feel up to explaining myself. He actually slapped me, maddened by my detachment. Suddenly, there was a knock at the door. Martha's girlfriend was trying to kill herself and had slashed her wrist. Sven rushed out to help her and, while they murmured softly in Swedish, Martha and I chatted peacefully in another room. Her detachment resembles mine. There are spots of the girl's blood on my denim jacket, oddly exciting.

JUNE 4
ISCHIA

This morning, for the first time since we've been here, it rained, drumming loudly on the tin roof of the terrace. The leaves of the fig trees are darker, and the sea lies flat, gray and resigned.

I wrote this just now:

> The rain flutters on the roof
> Like the wings of locusts
> The sea lies silent, robbed of its color
> And a mistaken cock demands the sun.

JUNE 6

Six cherries, and a green lizard, slinking like a harem girl, sampling them. The sea is very dark, red with rage. Fountains mount the walls. Sven is painting but I can't seem to write. Nature is too noisy and flirtatious.

JULY 3

Things have been altogether bad lately. Sven is getting hysterical about our sexual relationship, which he finds inadequate. We have painful arguments. I had an unhappy, demanding letter from my mother.

JULY 15

Last week a letter came from Susan, saying "I am in Paris. Meet me at Notre Dame." She gives no address and writes: "I cannot see you with my husband's knowledge." She has obviously, foolishly told him about our connection, my influence on her, and so on; so, of course, he never wants to hear of me again. Too much talking—and I have done it often—always complicates things. And then there have been so many missed opportunities in my life. Peggy [Tolk Watkins] accused me of having "no sense of timing," always leaving too early or arriving too late.

JULY 30
ROME

Rome, Rome, such magnificence! Where to begin? I could fill an entire notebook with the things we've seen, the excitements we've felt, the exaltation of it all!

I will try to condense it and tell its splendor without too much detail . . .

First, there is St. Peter's, on its grand piazza with the two great fountains flaunting their plumes of spray in the sun. Then there is the Vatican, with its miles of surreal corridors cluttered with cherubs, mermaids, wreaths, urns, leaves. The Sistine chapel;

its Michelangelo ceiling with his erotic young men and muscled women.

Peaches and ice cream in a tiny, sunstruck park.

The Pantheon trying to be Christian and the Piazza Navona, with its Bernini fountains representing the four great rivers—Nile, Ganges, Danube, and Rhine. A long-necked, small-headed horse like an elegant woman, a heavy, hunched lion, snakes, palm trees, and dolphins catching the shining water in their mouths. The color of the place: gold, green, black. Shade and sunlight.

We roamed small streets to the Palazzo Borghese (Borgias everywhere), with its garden furnished in imitation antiquities, very cool and green. Then off to take showers and make love in a public bathhouse.

In late afternoon, we climbed the Palatine Hill to look out over the ruins. In the square at the top, designed by Michelangelo, there is a moving equestrian statue, the rider curly-haired and bearded, a beautiful man.

Spent the evening with two boys from Ischia, ate well, and looked for the night life in the "artists' quarter" but didn't find it.

Yesterday we visited a marvelous old church in a working class neighborhood, Sta. Maria en Trastevere, with its mosaics of sheep, doves, and large-eyed faces. In the Jewish quarter we were followed by children crying "Shalom," shrieking and laughing. One little girl asked timidly if we were Jewish.

Last night we strolled to Piazza di Spagna, where Keats died in a large yellow house. Sat on the Via del Corso watching the beautiful whores passing by. Beauty is everywhere in this city. Then to the Forum, where we listened to Bach's *St. Matthew Passion*. What sky; what light on the green trees and gray pillars! It was like a dream, with the tall, golden music over everything.

This afternoon, at the invitation of a priest, Don Umberto, we went to see a special fresco in a convent. An old nun led us through, ringing a little bell to warn others that strangers were passing. It made me feel dirty, like a leper. We could hear the high, cool voices of the nuns, chanting.

Now it is night, and we are in the youth hostel, full of chattering young girls. The room where I sleep is empty. I am alone with twenty beds.

AUGUST 1
SIENNA

Hitchhiked from Rome. On our way out of the city, we met a red-haired man in a dirty black coat with a grimy bag slung over his shoulder. He asked if he could travel with us, but of course, we said no. A truck stopped for us and took him too a short way. Then we tried to shake him again. It was high noon, in a shadeless burning asphalt road. A man stopped, thinking I was alone, and angrily took both of us. At the edge of Viterbo we started to walk. Sven's sandal had broken and flapped pitifully on his long, dirty foot. A truck came by, and I almost didn't bother to hail it, but it stopped for us and there was the red-haired man, looking down at us reproachfully.

"Why didn't you want us to go together from Rome?" he asked, as we climbed aboard.

We explained that three were harder to find rides for, but he went on talking. He told us he had been in France, *senza documenti*, and in the army and was heading to Milano to look for work. Then his story changed. He was going to France or Germany.

We ate bread and cheese together and then lay down on the dusty truck bed. He watched me through slitted eyes from his corner and when we passed through an alley of trees, commented, "*Fresca, eh?*" When the truck stopped for a break, he helped me down, putting one hand carefully on my left breast. His arms were very strong.

Later, we picked up a young German couple. The boy was talkative but the girl sat silent. The red-haired man tried to chat with them, but they obviously were wary of him.

A fourth time, the driver stopped for a young German who had been thrown from his motorcycle. The men lifted him by his arms, bloody and gasping for breath, like a crucified one lowered from the cross. He smoked a cigarette and spoke to no one. The red-haired man wanted to know if he had his "papers." He seemed thrilled by the novel turn his voyage had taken, toward his being part of a group of young adventurous foreigners.

We left the injured boy in a small village, where there was, hopefully, a doctor, and the truck dropped us a little farther on where a sign said "35 Km to Sienna." We decided to take a bus and told the red-haired man, who turned suddenly cold as though we had once more rejected him, although he took the bus as well. He didn't speak to us again.

The Sienna cathedral is a wonder, striped black-and-white marble, with pink touches, lovely beasts spread over its façade, and a campanile with six arched windows growing larger as they climb. Inside the cathedral, there are gold angels and crystal chandeliers, hanging high beneath the blue and gold ceilings like diamond birds. Delicious!

AUGUST 4
FIRENZE

It is very hot. We have been walking and walking. Fell in love with the David all over again and a beautiful little Cretan goddess in the Etruscan Museum. She is ceramic, with long black hair, naked thrusting breasts, and a serpent in each hand.

We sat in a café, and somehow my skirt caught

fire, and Sven put it out with his bare hands. Tattered, I went looking for a tailor. A man sent me up a flight of stairs, where two middle-aged prostitutes mended my skirt. I was sitting in my panties when a man came up, and they shut him in another room, saying there was "*una bella Americana nuda*" present and that he would have to wait. I saw him peeping, grinning, behind the door. The women were very kind and would not accept the money I offered . . .

AUGUST 8
VENEZIA

Tonight, walking through a dark alley, we heard tango music played on an accordion coming from a café window. Old people sat on chairs, cats slept, and a young couple danced with what looked like passion. Watched a handsome blond gondolier passing below us in his pale blue sailor shirt, tight black pants, and yellow straw hat with a red ribbon, moving like a dancer.

Somehow, though, all this water is slightly oppressive.

Today we rented a rowboat and floated along the Grand Canal when, suddenly, it began to pour. We sheltered under the Rialto Bridge, soaked and helpless.

In Florence, I ran into Marion Rothman, a lesbian from Black Mountain . . . not a very pleasant en-counter. Then we went to visit Peggy's friend, Lucia [Vernarelli], who has an apartment here. She is very beautiful with an almost classical Greek head and immense, bulging, pale green eyes. I have a powerful reaction to people from my Peggy past. Somehow, they intimidate me with a glamour and sophistica-tion that I lack. Sven is annoyed by this.

BACK IN ISCHIA

I had a brief flirtation with a pretty Australian girl in Venice. I was late for our date at the Piazza San Marco, and she was gone, or perhaps hadn't come. My lesbian past seems to hang around me like an aura, an aura I would like to lose.

We hitched to Ravenna for the wonderful mosaics and then to Arezzo, with an Italian who drove much too fast, rushing down narrow mountain roads and sharp curves with macho ego.

The Della Francescas are in a drab church where they blaze in a dazzle of blue sky, shot with lively clouds and sturdy men on horses. The men are fierce and primitive looking, with wild, stringy hair.

Spent the night in Perugia, an old town built on the top of a conical mountain like a great stone hat. Below it are wide sweeping plains dotted with trees and houses. In the morning we caught a truck going straight to Rome.

It was a long trip in the hot sun through the beautiful Umbrian countryside. In Rome again, but differently. Our time is limited by my journey back to the States in September, my first return since my new life here with Sven. I am a little afraid.

SEPTEMBER 20, 1951
ABOARD THE *ATLANTIC*

This morning we docked in Barcelona, and walking through the ripe, dirty streets, I felt an intense love for the place. Near the port a boy called out "Greta Garbo!" I had a few pesetas and gave them to the sad, sickly-looking children who did not beg. One little boy, in a girl's dress with cropped head, shouted gaily and laughed at me.

OCTOBER 3, 1951
NEW YORK

Words "I do not like you," written on the wall of the el station at Canal Street. Men calling after me, "Hey, Miss!" as I roamed a bit drunk. Cigarettes and beer and brandy and my sad mother, all mixed up in my head like poison. Such guilt, like the pursuing hound in the poem.

NOVEMBER 15
ABOARD THE *ILE-DE-FRANCE*

Now I really must write about New York. Something, cowardice or lethargy, kept me from doing it there. I am in a single cabin, with a silver vase of red roses, gift of my mother, and the sound of the sea-peace.

Most wonderful element of the visit was my reconciliation with my sister. She allowed me to read her journals from the TB sanatorium, powerful and tragic, and we found each other again.

Spent last evening with the "old crowd"—Helen, Willi [Reynolds], Blanche [Sherwood], Lucia—a community of women, a strange little group, with its unspoken intimacies, passions, delicate games. They are a bit too exquisite for my rough taste.

NOVEMBER 16
AT SEA

The porthole is open, and if I stand on the couch I can see the rippling wall of water along the ship's side and the far gray line of horizon. Sitting on deck before, all snug in my red chair and plaid blanket, I felt very happy at the prospect of seeing Sven, my tall, tender lover. The roses in my cabin are big with decay. Tomorrow they will fall. I realize now how *shy* Bobbie and I have been with each other after our warm and solid childhood.

NOVEMBER 19
ABOARD SHIP

Last night was the gala, and I was seated at the purser's table. We had champagne and sat apart from the rest of tourist class. Madame X [Katherine Gravet], whom I have been admiring, was also at the table. It turns out she is a painter, married to the uncle of a boy I knew at Black Mountain. I will see her in Paris.

Yesterday afternoon there was a movie in the lounge, a French film noir, a serial killer thing which I enjoyed immensely. That, along with the duck à l'orange, champagne, and my "period," produced a terrifying dream about lesbians, sadism, and Sven. I awoke shivering and confused. The only amusing part was that I was sitting at a table with the Windsors and the King and Queen of England. Clearly, I was ridiculously flattered by last night's invitation.

DECEMBER 13
PARIS

I spent the day in bed with an inexplicable, short-lived fever. Strangely, almost a year ago, Sven was ill and I nursed him. It is all very different now because our life together has survived the separation.

DECEMBER 20
PARIS

It is a cold, rainy day. I sit close to the stove, soaking up warmth. On the roof, across our ruined courtyard, there is a calico cat washing himself. Behind him the sky is blank except for a few puffs of gray smoke from a factory chimney. Handel's *Messiah* is on the radio.

"And who shall abide the day of His coming . . ." I am reading *Mademoiselle de Maupin* and yearning for adventure and abandon.

DECEMBER 30

It's a rainy day, and I sit by the stove nursing the impetigo sores on my legs and telling Sven, "I want to live!" He feels contempt for my scattered desires. He is fundamentally practical and peaceful, devoted to his art, complacent as a child. While I, foolishly, need something marvelous to happen every day, like *Steppenwolf* or the cavalier in *Mademoiselle de Maupin*. When I wake up in the morning, I have a feeling of expectation . . . maybe something wonderful will happen. By late afternoon it is gone, and unless we have plans for the evening, I descend into boredom and hopelessness. I am the sort of person who cannot leave the house without a faint tickle of excitement. I cannot look at a beautiful face on the street or in the metro without a small frisson of joy. Sven sees this as stupid and childish, and his disapproval finally embarrasses me and makes me feel hostile toward him.

Last night I played my sister's George Shearing record, and it brought me back to her room, with its two tall windows, rain pouring down outside, the divan and the small objects of her life. That room was kind to me before she herself was. I found an odd "play" in one of her notebooks about two sisters, "the one who loved women" and "the one who became a whore," each on an opposite corner of the stage conducting monologues about their painful love for each other.

JANUARY 1, 1952
PARIS

Peggy [Tolk-Watkins] is here. She tells me she loves me, but now I understand what that means. She flirts ostentatiously with me in front of Sven, which drives him wild. The other night at the Dôme, with Martin there to add to the confusion, the tension was horrible. At home, Sven was furious and vicious, pushing me out of bed, saying, "Go to her, go to Peggy," and then weeping with rage, regret, and love.

How different they are, these loves. Peggy and Sven cannot even speak to each other; they have different languages.

It is spring and my heart wakes up after this long, horrible winter. I am attracted to other people, a sign of energy.

Another piece of mine will appear in *New Story* next month. And the only one I wrote this winter was rejected by *Partisan Review.* I am feeling very dry and limited.

Soon it will be two years that I have been with Sven in Europe, and I will be twenty-three with so little to show for it. Time flies by, and already, unbelievably, I have much gray hair!

FEBRUARY 1952

George VI, the king of England, died today. The Princess Elizabeth is now Queen Elizabeth II. In a café WC in the Avenue Messine, someone wrote that he liked to suck pussy: Sucer a fond une jolie chatte.

I am writing these things down to reassure myself that there is still a world outside of my limited one—a world of friends, kings, lust . . .

FEBRUARY 20

Well, I am quite alright after a month of hypochondriacal panic. But misfortune is still with us. The other night there was a fire in the closet, and all my pretty things—blouses of velvet and silk and soft red jersey—all of them are gone.

And now Sven has a paralysis (Bell's Palsy) on one side of his face. Poor sweet thing. He looks like a puzzled animal with small wet eyes and a comically distorted mouth. It frightens and worries me but, *au fond*, I am undisturbed. Such is the ego, the horrid little jewel concerned only with itself.

And I have beautiful friends now . . . Martin and Katherine. Even thinking of giving myself a birthday party.

It has snowed again, and diamond icicles reflect the pale sun.

An enchanting afternoon. Life flowers now. Friends . . .

I wash clothes. Evening comes. My birthday is next week I told Sven I want a ring.

MARCH 29, 1952

Two years ago today, I sailed for Europe. Three days ago, I was twenty-three. Sven gave me a beautiful ring, a large rose-orange agate in a heavy silver setting.

On my birthday, we went to the Comédie-Française and sat in a box near the stage in the small red-and-gold theater.

How love hurts, I realize. How it confines one, like being indoors all the time. Even if you like the inside, there is always the temptation to look outside at those passing figures in the street with their mysterious otherness. Oh, the curse of imagination!

APRIL 2

I rode my bicycle over to visit Martin in his new place. It is on the top floor of a small hotel—two rooms with skylights and a low slanting ceiling. A view of house tops and chimneys. He showed me his new paintings. They are of women, erotic dreams, ideal nude couples strolling through trees and fields of flowers. One painting, which he called *Motherhood*, was a portrait of the plump young Irish actress I think he is in love with. She was to have come to see him today, but when she was late, he came with me to the Luxembourg Gardens. We sat on the edge of the pond and watched the children's tiny boats. When the rain came on, we walked back to Montparnasse. Two pigeons made love in the air, very quickly, and one flew away. "Il en a eu assez," Martin said bitterly.

APRIL 22
BRUSSELS

Sven's paintings hang beautifully in the Galerie ex Libris, but almost no one comes in to see them. We sit in the empty gallery while crowds pass in the grand'place but few come in. And of course, nothing has sold, and we will be utterly broke and have to forget a trip to Spain. The show now seems to have been a big mistake.

Sunday we hitched to Bruges, an old town of canals and bridges and small brick houses with step roofs. The brick looks soft, changes with the weather, is mostly a reddish gold.

The little canals are lined with leaning trees, now in blossom. Sun and moss float on the slow water.

We visited a convent called a béguinage, home to a very strict order famous for making lace.

The cloister walls open on a tiny lake called Minnewater, a favorite resting place for swans. After breakfast at the hostel, we walked there and watched them performing their daily toilettes. They preened their feathers and then walked into the water. Suddenly, as we were turning away, there was a great flapping of wings and a line of them half rose into the air. Their enormous wings seemed to strain to lift them, but their passion, the need to fly, was beautiful. Since I am getting the "curse," it almost made me cry.

MAY 1
PARIS

Today is the *Fête du Muguet* (Festival of the Lilies of the Valley), a soft, rainy kind of day. Martin brought me some of the flowers, and their sweet perfume, the sound of an accordion playing nearby, created a delicious sensation of Paris; its very nature. How happy I am here now! I love the cafés spilling over into the street while I fly by on my bicycle.

MAY 25

Last night I went with Peggy, Blanche, Willi, and Gio to the American jazz club, Chez Inez. I wore a tight white sleeveless shirt and a black velvet skirt and felt beautiful. I feel very secure in my new life, detached from Peggy and the past.

[Peggy was my first female lover. I was eighteen, attending summer session at Black Mountain College in North Carolina. She was in her middle twenties, a boyish woman wearing Brooks Brothers shirts, tight levis, and a general air of sophistication that made me recognize my own lack of it. She introduced me to Djuna Barnes, Proust, Bessie Smith—a whole hip homosexual culture of which I was unaware. I followed her to San Francisco. She taught me a lot about cruelty and ambivalence.

Early in our relationship she told me, "You're not a lesbian; you're just in love with me." I know now that she was right.]

I came home about two a.m. in a shaky old taxi. Sven was not feeling well, mean and unhappy, saying nasty things. I coldly let him make love to me. The light was pale and fainting around five, when we finally fell asleep.

JUNE 20
IBIZA, SPAIN

I am sitting half in sunlight on our little balcony in the Calle de la Virgen. At the end of our street the sea ripples lazily in a light wind. This is a street of fishermen, children, chickens, cats, and whores. The two brothels are here, and I see the women strolling from one house to the other, great-breasted, with polished fingernails. The madam dresses neatly in black. Her dark hair is cropped and she wears a gold cocktail ring and a watch to match. She has a handsome, scowling, middle-aged face. There are young ones too—one skinny adolescent who sings and snaps her fingers—and a big, dumb-looking girl whose too-tight shirt gapes open over her breasts. A fat, bleach-blonde with shapeless legs goes between the houses with American cigarettes and a thermometer in her hand.

There are also the cats, skinny and ruffled, striped, black and tailless. Mostly, they sleep curled in sunny spots against the houses. Sometimes a fight breaks out, with much yowling and hissing, and the little dog on the balcony with the fishnet curtains barks once, a reprimand.

The children live in the street as well. Their bare feet scatter orange peels, fruit pits, a rotten crab, fish heads in the dust. Their mothers shout, "Manolo! Juanito!" Ibicencos love noise. The children are absorbed; they don't hear the calls. A boy on the balcony across the street has just glued five little green tickets on the wall of his house using a lot of spit. He says nothing to his grandmother, who sews at a table under a faint yellow bulb.

A little girl, perhaps three, comes out in a petticoat with mismatched shoes, both too big for her. She has tiny gold hoops in her ears and short, golden-brown hair. She sits down on the doorstep of her house and pees, smiling at the little dark stream that rolls over the step and stains the ground. She pokes her finger into it and stirs. No one cleans the street here. Fish heads, fruit peels, shit remain. The chickens eat some of it, the children play with it, and what remains is swept away by the sun and air. Already, the little stream of piss has vanished.

JUNE 22
IBIZA

I am sitting on the long stone jetty leading to the lighthouse, midway between land and sea, on this narrow, sun-warmed slab of stone. The wind ruffles my hair and the pages of this diary.

A small, monkey-faced soldier has sidled up near me, mumbling *guapa*. He stares, grinning and curious, at my silence and preoccupation. More soldiers are gathering—bored—tan flies around me. My calm puzzles them. I am beginning to feel annoyed, so I move to another spot. They follow, singing some kind of rhumba.

Now I am down on the lower quay with my back against the lighthouse wall. There is less wind here. The water slaps against the stone, and four little sailboats scatter over the choppy green like scraps of paper.

There are too many of these young soldiers in the garrison here. They are terribly bored. They should be at work on farms or building houses instead of loafing around in their ugly, ill-fitting uniforms.

JULY 1

Paradise is being spoiled. I watch helplessly as waves of annoyance mount around me, noisy, intrusive people, too much concern with food and cooking, Sven and I arguing constantly about small things. Sex is not good either.

July 3
The *Corrida*

Tiny young men wearing velvet, silver, and sequins, pink stockings and soft black slippers. Their bodies are shapely, sinuous.

But oh, the poor bull! He prances out of the enclosure, magnificent and angry, his long, curving horns smacking blindly against the walls. The matador, dressed in pale blue and silver, holds bright ribbon-wrapped spears in his hands and dances a slow pavane toward him. He holds the spears high and plunges them into the bull's neck as he runs past. They are hooked and hang from the flesh. The bull is furious. The matador dances toward him again, smiling proudly. He plants two more spears and again two more. Blood streams down the bull's black hide. Then the young man removes his hat, a sign of respect, and hides the sword he holds in a small, red cape. The bull dashes at the cape many times while the man steps nimbly aside. When, at last, the bull stands still in fury and bewilderment, the man raises the sword in one arm and sinks it deep into his neck. But the first hit is not enough. Blood pours from the animal's nostrils and eyes. He staggers and coughs. The bloody sword is pulled out by its hilt and plunged into him again. The other *toreros,* with their folded pink-and-gold cloaks, stand around like onlookers at an accident. The crowd shouts.

"*Dale la muerte!*" Kill him! The matador strikes again. The bull's soft gray mouth hangs open; his eyes roll back. He falls finally, very slowly. The men in their costumes look stupid and helpless—abashed. It is not a glorious death. Then, a sturdy horse is brought into the arena, chained to the carcass and led out, dragging the bloody body through the dust. The band strikes up triumphantly but it was *malo,* and the crowd whistles derisively.

Today the café served steak . . .

JULY 6

There is an American woman here, Caroline Delteil [married to the Surrealist poet Joseph Delteil] the sister of Sven's friends Catherine Dudley and Dorothy Harvey [biographer of Theodore Dreiser]. They are American aristocrats and confirmed expatriates. Caroline is the person who discovered Josephine Baker in a club in Chicago and brought her to Paris! She is beautiful, with the face of a sensitive pug dog—bulging, anxious eyes, a strong chin. She has cropped gray hair and large hands. She admires Poe, Emily Dickinson, Melville, and is writing a novel. "I leave out all the words I can," she says. I have a sort of crush on her. How different are our Americas— mine, second-generation immigrants'; hers, the old WASP stock with its inherent privileges.

JULY 7

Today is my sister's birthday. I sit on our balcony, cooled by a light, salty breeze. The street lights stay on all day, artificial pearls against the blue. A young whore passes with curlers in her hair. The madam goes by in a black dress printed with red flowers. She turns her dark, clever eyes up at me.

JULY 9

Sven has a fever and I have a chest cold. He is lying on the white sheets, and his skin is very tan and beautiful. Our tiny black kitten sleeps next to him.

JULY 10

I still have a cold and a voice like an old hag. The weather is muggy, and last night a huge black cloud blotted out moon and stars. At El Kiosco, the big spear fisherman stared at me with his small, hot eyes.

Sven got a letter from a girl in New York, whom he met while I was in the States. She wrote, "How rare for people to be so close in such a short time. How I regret . . . etc." She talks about returning to Europe in the fall. It made me very jealous, but then, he *did* show it to me.

JULY 13

Last night I had fever and went to bed with aspirin in a *vin chaud*.

This morning, Caroline came and made tea and sat with me, talking about Dos Passos, whom she knows. She again told me how beautiful I am. "I used to have feet as good as yours." Actually, she is marvelous looking. At sixty, she is straight and sturdy, her short gray hair combed back from her cat-like face, the great bulging green eyes, small nose, curved mouth. She is a snob and a lady. We have the same birthday, March 26, but she was born in 1892!

JULY 14

We went out into the cool gray morning and sat at the café watching the moving boats at high tide, the swarms of gulls. Then we went to a doctor, who says I have bronchitis and should stay in bed for two days. Sick in summer! How hateful! I love Ibiza, the sea's swishing broom, the immense night skies and the lives that grow strong and beautiful here, against all odds, like our kitten who has survived so much abuse.

JULY 15

It is the Feast of Santa Carmen. The street is hung with blue paper pennants adorned with silver stars and moons. They rustle in the wind like leaves. There is also an arch made of palm branches and flowers, and hung with oars and life savers. Tonight, after the procession, there will be dancing.

JULY 16

Caroline and her sister Catherine were here this morning. Caroline left the MS of her novel, which I have been reading all day. It is called *Lighthouse Blues* and is wonderful.

JULY 20

I am on the pier with our kitten, Echo, reading Proust. The clouded sky is spattered with gold and the bay is wild. Sails rush by. Also, the stink of the nearby urinal. Some children stand timidly around me, watching me make blue signs on this white paper, hoping to see a picture. But I make only words.

An old man sits near. He has coarse black hair like grass; one of his eyes is glassy white, the other dark. He rolls a cigarette for himself, and in the somber rock of his face, a flame flickers. One boy has a white bandage around his head, and a little girl with curly hair wears a tin bottle cap pinned to her dress.

JULY 30

On Saturday, we went to the tiny island of Formentera, which sits under a dazzling, cloudless sky across the bay. There are *salinas* there, basins with dams behind them in which the sea water evaporates, leaving bloody-looking crystal pools of salt. The salt turns the earth around it into a dead crust and eats the rocks, first blackening them, sucking out the iron. Then it coats them with mold. The pools give off a shocking stench, like rotten meat. The rising vapors clear the air so that there is never a cloud above the island, just a brilliant, empty blue.

AUGUST 13

This morning I swam from the rocks at Los Molinos. It was very rough, hard to climb out.

I felt a sort of delirium in being beaten and choked by the waves, clinging to the rocks until at last, with all my strength, I pulled clear.

The kitten nibbles at great pink and orange flowers in a big, tin cup. She looks like a tiny panther in a Rousseau jungle. The two pink roses among them are round and delicate, heavy on their stems, like breasts.

AUGUST 24

We walked up to the old town this evening to visit Catherine. Her sister Dorothy is here with her daughter Anne, a timid creature in her thirties with large blue eyes and a slim little body. She paints surprisingly strong, intimate pictures—portraits and stilllifes. She has a soft, tentative voice, like a Henry James heroine.

AUGUST 25

Suddenly, it feels like autumn. The heat has fled, leaving a pale fluttering shell behind. Shadows come early to our street. When thunder sounded, a little boy shouted, "*Oiga! Escucha!*" and asked what it was. He is not normal. He has a soft face with a small mustache, like Proust. The grocer calls him "*Pobrecito*" and gives him a piece of candy. He fluttered into our house this morning wearing a too-small white shirt with the initials "RM" embroidered on it. He rolls on the ground, laughing.

SEPTEMBER 2

My mother has some kind of skin disease on her face. She writes, "Probably it is nothing serious," but they don't know yet. I feel the terror in the words.

SEPTEMBER 7

No news from Mother. If she were not in the world anymore, what would freedom mean to me? Oh, my strong peasant-bodied mother, how have I wounded you?

OCTOBER 12
PARIS

Back in my beautiful city in its autumn clothes! The trees by the river sing in yellow, Paris, the youths' golden hair.

I am trying hard to find a job. We need a place to live. It is difficult, but *quand même, c'est Paris!* Bernie Frechtman, Annette Michelson's lover and Genet's translator, says, "One's life is *lighter* away from one's one country."

My sister has had an abortion and wants to come here. It would be good for her, but then, poor Mom and Dad, all alone . . .

I saw a man today who wants me to work for him, ghostwriting. He was kindly and flirtatious, reminding me of my father, and, oddly, his name was also Philip.

OCTOBER 28

We are in a new room, still in the fourteenth arrondissement. It has two windows—one on the street, rue Maurice Ripoche (such an ugly name!) and the other on a dingy little courtyard where a family lives. Some of them look Chinese—a lively little silk-haired boy. The women are fat and sad-looking, but the small Chinese father looks young. It reminds me a bit of San Francisco.

On the street side, there are also many children and a café with the classic name, Au Bon Coin. Downstairs from us is a restaurant, Café Bucarest, run by an oily-looking Rumanian and his big blonde wife.

We had bananas and yogurt for breakfast.

OCTOBER 29

Sven came home very late last night. Dinner was ready, and I waited and got worried and went out to look for him. It began to rain, and I sat in our room, cold and sweating. He finally returned at nine o'clock and at first I was glad to see him. But then a high wind of anger swept down on me. I went out into the rainy dark, blown along by rage. And then it faded away, and I began feeling good about being by myself at night in the street. I considered going to a dyke bar, but that seemed a bit drastic. So I went to the Dôme where people looked surprised at seeing me alone. I felt good.

Later, in bed, I began to bleed. Waking up with a pain in my belly, I put my fingers into my vagina. A soft sort of warm liquid was there. Sven put a large piece of drawing paper under me to protect the mattress.

This afternoon, alone in the studio, I read some old letters from Mimi, Sven's ex-wife. Strangely, I felt nothing, no jealousy, just somehow pity for both of them.

November 1, Toussaint (All Saints' Day)

This room becomes more and more significant to me. Its two views, the street and the courtyard, seem to represent two "outlooks" on life.

On the street side, people pass with umbrellas, dogs, bags; pigeons play in puddles; cars stop and start. Some people seem self-conscious, as if aware that someone is watching them. (I am.)

On the courtyard side, there are the shiny roof tiles, the pathetically wet cluster of pink baby clothes hanging in the window, the pots and pans on the sink.

In between is this room, mine alone in the day while Sven works in his studio. It is waiting to be filled with words and memories. Our relationship has reached a stage where we don't need to be together all the time and can spend our days apart, knowing we will find each other at the end.

DECEMBER 1

Sven left this morning for a week in London. I have made a web of appointments to fill the time and keep me from missing him. I am reading *Albertine disparue*, which seems appropriate to the feeling of loss. As always, I care most for Sven when he is absent.

DECEMBER 19

Martin is really leaving for Germany on Monday, not to return. He is coming soon to have dinner with us, and I feel a deep disappointment. After all, we've been flirting for so long, and now it's too late!

DECEMBER 20

Dreamed all night about Martin. We were making love.

I still don't dare to write everything in these pages. Sven peeks.

DECEMBER 28

What Bernie Frechtman said the other night about great writing needing an element of violence seems true. I would like to write a story full of it.

My sister has had a nose job and is using a stage name, "Stefanie David." Will I recognize her when I see her? But, of course, the sweet round brown-velvet eyes will still be the same.

JANUARY 1, 1953

Last night there was a party at Jan and Marjorie's. I got crazy drunk and a little Dutch girl with a lovely scarred face said I had made a pass at her. It snowed.

Today we slept, and I dreamed about Peggy, Susan, all sorts of people. I think, suddenly, "Oh my God, I'll soon be twenty-four!" Just heard a radio broadcast from Times Square. My heart is fat with nostalgia.

JANUARY 5

More and more, I am getting to understand the mechanics of our relationship. It all hinges on whether or not we make love. When we do, he is sweet, generous, and indulgent with me. When we don't, he is cold and mean. And I am increasingly aware of my own sexual cycle. Its highest point is the week after my period. Then I become absolutely indifferent for two weeks (without unusual stimulus). Then I revive, the week before the "curse." Sven's feelings for me follow this course.

Raymond [Mason] is around a lot now because Mimi is away. He is really a beautiful man. But he can be annoyingly pedantic; he theorizes about everything. However, his description of living alone was exactly right—how the room freezes and one needs any company one can get.

Last night I said "English fairies" in describing Sven when I meant to say "Swedish pirates." I suppose I sometimes do see him like that when he whines and wiggles and pleads for sex.

Just finished *Madame Bovary*, a tremendous book! Emma longs for adventure, glamour, beauty. She dreams it but is made to accept mediocre substitutes: the river bank as a seaport, the little housemaid as a servant. Her lovers are all creatures of her will; their encounters of her fantasy. She is a life-artist, but how her material resists her! Finally, only her death is real—self-created, horrible, and dramatic!

JANUARY 13

Yellow mimosas in the yellow pitcher, their lovely perfume. I bought them from a woman at the corner of rue Daguerre. Her thin, young face was red with cold. She wanted me to take two bunches for fifty francs and when I said I only had enough for one, she exclaimed, "*Ah, chérie, vous êtes comme moi, alors, pauvre . . .*" I was touched by her acceptance.

JANUARY 27

I open my window to let in the cold breath of the street and the sound of buses passing on *avenue du Maine*, the cry of a mother, "*Viens, viens, chéri,*" the growl and pant of trucks, the sweet, quiet presence of this little street, my Paris!

My mother has written, "Come home. Your father is ill," and Bobbie (Steffi) writes, "Dad is quite sick." She includes a photo of herself, an elegant, red-lipped, red-nailed girl, seated on the arm of a chair occupied by a fat, bald, Jewish businessman—a girl to have a good time with in Miami. How awful!

Of course, I may have to go home. This comes in the midst of a new period of hopes and dreams for me and Sven. If I go, it will be for two months again. To stay longer would be dangerous, and I will return to my love and Europe in the spring.

FEBRUARY 17
LONDON

We had a frightening Channel crossing. I was so sick I wasn't even afraid of the tremendous waves. Now, we are here in a luxurious apartment with rich, dull, sophisticated people, the awful food, the bus rides, the squares—Cadogan, Eaton—the parks full of rain, like great sponges.

I am working on the de Sade translation at an old carved desk, in a room full of rich deep carpets.

And then there is Elizabeth at the gallery, her sly flirtatiousness, her curiosity. She is disappointed when I say, "I don't like women," only individuals, but then renews hope when I hint at past connections. She asks me to send her a copy of *The World of Women Lovers* from Paris. I must remember not to put a return address on the envelope. I don't trust her to be discreet, and it would be awful for Sven if there was gossip.

MARCH 12
PARIS

Sven is still in London, and it is strange to be alone. I am working hard at the Sade. I even dreamt about it last night.

Raymond has been over twice. He is cold and

warm at once; very nervous. Tonight Herta [Hauss-man, a German painter] came. She is dark and hand-some in very masculine clothes, hair like Peggy's. She was in an all-female French internment camp for two years. She says extreme things like "I would vomit if I had to eat that banana!" which she had brought herself. I put an orange in her hand, and she snatched at it, as if I would take it back.

The other night, I was at Sam Wolfenstein's, drinking Pernod. No longer the lonely, bitter one, he is married and has a son. His hatred of Jews (self-hatred) is poisonous.

I hope to finish the translation tomorrow and be free to go out to the Dôme in the evening. A little English girl named Percy came over this morning. She seems to have a crush on me. Delighted at my in-vitation (immediately regretted) to come back some evening. She borrowed my copy of *Nightwood*. [It was never returned].

A beautiful evening walk on the quay by Châte-let—river green, sky violet, trees dark like hair, and globes of light, pearl earrings. An evening out of Proust. We bought old postcards, three francs apiece, four for ten.

Soon it will be my birthday, soon Easter, soon three years of Europe and Sven!

MARCH 26, 1953

My birthday! Caroline's too. She will celebrate with us. Had a letter from Nanna yesterday: "Happy birthday; be a birthday child always. And a rose on paper with brown eyes. And always love me and always be very good like a red-painted boat, leaning to and standing on grass with one foot . . ."

APRIL 4

Listening to *La Voix de l'Amérique*. My parents are buying a house in Miami. Jazz, jazz . . . Suddenly, I miss it very much . . . the craziness, the sickness, the sexiness, the badness. "Black, black, black is the color of my true love's hair . . ." America . . .

APRIL 10

As usual, I talked too much to Herta, the German painter, about my childhood, schooling, New York, Black Mountain—finally letting it all hang out. She is friendly, unperturbed, but a few minutes later tells me she loves boys.

APRIL 23, REAL SPRING!

Romaine came into our lives again yesterday with her handsome, classic profile, strong legs—still walking with a cane. Sven has a strange reaction to her, probes and prods her clumsily I think. She is a bit *distraite*; flirts with me. Will she come again?

Sunday, we went to Auvers with Herta. I hope she doesn't fall in love with Sven, and yet, I like her. Visited the graves of Theo and Vincent, both covered in the same black leaves. Behind the cemetery there is the wide, pale landscape into which he painted color and madness.

It's hot! Spent the afternoon in the Luxembourg gardens, reading and watching the children. I feel a strange uneasiness alone in a park. Memories of Central Park, perhaps, the exhibitionists?

Seen:

Infant rabbits, two white, one brown, suckling at a great white, rose-nosed mother, who stares up into the roof of sun.

A little girl with a small white face, long, untidy dark hair, dancing to say goodbye on stick legs, waving a hand like a butterfly wing.

Herta, standing in her big dark room, smoking, in a pitifully pretty shirt. Her humility, warmth, and lovingness. Since that day, saying "lesbian" in an aware way.

A tiny messenger boy on a tall, thin bicycle . . .

APRIL 29

Romaine again, the shadowy, the indistinct, leaning her cane against my thigh in the theater and moving her foot against it. Intentional? We share a cigarette in the dark. Herta was on the other side of me and Sven behind her. Later, Herta said Romaine is *diabolique,* like the film. I have no way to contact her if I wanted to. Better so.

Second letter from Elizabeth in London.

MAY 2

Yesterday I went to Herta's. It was an eccentric, blowy afternoon. She had been sleeping. She showed me some sketches of myself. *"Je te dessine tout le temps,"* she said. One was a nude, delicate, flowers in the hair; another was hard and violent. Funny how easily I gave up on her, thought I had shocked or bored her, when perhaps all the time . . .

What's important is not always betraying these things to others.

MAY 6

Daddy's birthday.

I must somehow get to Munich to visit Nanna.

JUNE 11

ON THE TRAIN BACK TO PARIS FROM MUNICH

I have a headache. Nanna left me on the station platform with a quick kiss, and, like a sparrow taking flight, was gone. The sky is heavy over Bavaria.

I have a lump in my vagina, as big as a plum. We went to a doctor, who had a picture of himself on his desk in an SS uniform. He said it is a cyst and he could cut it right out. Naturally, I refused his help— a Nazi! I will see a doctor in Paris.

And in Nymphenburg we sat in the shade on a green bench, watching the swans converse slowly down the stream, ducks darting past like arrows, ducklings running on the water.

Nanna—fear and love. "I don't care anymore about anything," she says, strong but self-devouring. And me, with my Achilles'-heel vagina . . . love and death together.

What will Sven say?

JUNE 17

What a mess! Should I go to see Herta? Should I go to the prefecture? Should I write my mother, buy a cake?

JUNE 21

This "thing" with Herta, innocent as it is, gets worse and worse. Sven is being nasty. We are afraid to walk on the street together, afraid of meeting him.

It's gonorrhea! What the French call the *chaude-pisse*. I have a constant headache.

JUNE 22

It's a bad joke. I, the modest, the innocent, almost the chaste, to have the whore's disease!

I sleep the Sunday through. Why wake? Everything waits. Strangely, Sven seems to love me more. Guilt? I must have caught it from him, though he denies being unfaithful. The tests show he has it too, but in an asymptomatic form. We are both infected and getting antibiotics. Clearly, he lies . . .

JULY 6

At a party with Simon Vinkenhoog, the tall, blond Dutchman. He had passed out, sleeping with puffed-up red lips. I put a green leaf in his open white hand, a leaf Herta brought me from the garden. What a dance! Simon, Herta, Sven, me. I am afraid of touching, as if I were a leper.

When I go to the doctor for the injections into my labia, there is a curious excitement. Afterwards, I am in a strange, breathless condition . . . trembling. My face feels tight. Men seem to follow me and stare when I leave the doctor's office. My look of violation must attract them. I walk with my legs close together.

July 8

It is a day of cool, bright wind, sailing clouds. Oh, to be on the quay in Ibiza with each wavelet a pricking, silver pin! Here, Paris rumbles and groans. The sickness between my legs stays and stays. I may have to have surgery to remove the infected gland.

Herta came bringing snapdragons—pink, white and yellow. Already their petals are falling.

Bastille Day, 1953

Last night I danced in the street with Sven, with strangers, with Simon, while Herta searched for me in the wild, gay night. At the core of the hours, I felt the pitifulness of my condition.

Herta's is pitiful too. I just went to her place and found a damp note to me pinned to her gate in the rain. Last night someone read my palm. She said independence is the key to my character softened by a kind heart. "You've been independent since you were three!"

JULY 15

Thank God, the *fête* is over. I think if it went on any longer, one would go nuts . . . either from being out every night in the electric crowds, or from staying home, knowing that on distant boulevards, tall milk-skinned boys with gold hair and pale eyes (Simon) were out looking for love, as were shiny chocolate boys in white shirts and green scarves, and Raymond for example, in his pink shirt and rust-colored jacket, standing there in his own cold aura.

JULY 21

A man selling Bibles in a bar late at night, said to me, "*Jeunesse passe, mlle., jeunesse passe . . .*" warning me, I suppose, that I will die. We came home at five a.m. on the motorcycle, rushing past the Luxembourg Gardens, all pink and green, fresh as the flesh of a peach.

How beautiful the city was last night, the shimmering rooftops in the half moon, the clear stars, the field of chimneys like odd flowers! Finally, there has been a kiss between Herta and me. Her fresh, ripe lips are amazingly young and tender.

Sven and I are leaving on Friday. Peggy would say that I was "missing the boat again" with Herta but really, where can it go?

July 27
Auxerre

Seen:
A blonde farm girl, tall and strong, leading a big gray horse.

The slim bridge over the Yonne river full of clouds.

The cathedral—the insane, royal blue of the stained-glass windows.

The Mass—the tall, young man in the shadows, staring at me like a Stendhal character.

And, waiting for Sven in the *place de l'eglise*, two old ladies and a white-bearded man dressed in black, carrying their gloves; their silent, hidden lives.

August 4
Lacoste, Vaucluse France

In our new house—an ancient stone house bought for thirty-five US dollars. No electricity, no plumbing but beautiful. It is a fresh night . . . the lamp's tranquil hiss, music on the radio. Sven is so happy . . . it is honey to my heart.

August 8

A strange, dark wind, the mistral, this afternoon. It opens the thick heat; perhaps brings a storm. What a strange voyage I am on! Sven and I have been three years building this life, and now it is real . . . a stone house, terra cotta roof tiles, *our* house!?

AUGUST 9

Dreamed last night I was making love to Herta in my *father's* apartment (Mlle. Vinteuil in Proust?).She was a bit giggly or cynical. "*Tu n'arriveras pas*," she said, explaining that she had never come or made oral love with a woman. The dream was very real and unpleasant and exciting.

AUGUST 14

There are strikes all over France. No mail, no trains. No one can reach me now. It's a sort of contentment. Yesterday in Forcalquier, at a shop called *Le Clou*, there was a man talking about Saint-Rémy. I asked if he knew Diorka, Herta's old lover, and he did. He said my accent in French was like hers and that I resembled her. Lesbian lovers do tend to look alike. This happened once or twice with Peggy.

Afterward, we went to visit an old homosexual painter named Lucien Jacques. He lives in a tiny village far off the road. His house is full of curious objects, like a large, worm-eaten wooden bust of a young Roman, painted pink, with red lips and black curls. The place felt like a small fortress of memories. "*Je ne suis bien qu'ici,*" he said, I am only happy here.

Our kitchen is full of flies . . . loud buzzing and tickling. I am reading Lucien Jacques's French translation of Moby Dick. From the village comes a light sound of hammering; earlier a harmonica.

I had a strange dream last night. Nanna was discussing me, sitting on a couch with a young man. She said: "The artist must be already damned to be able to tell the truth without fear of damnation. Harriet is damned." Damned? What the fuck does it mean?

AUGUST 18
LACOSTE

I am having ferocious dreams. In this one, I am out all night with my "best friend" from my teens, Edith, who says, "We loved each other before but didn't know it."

Then I have another dream: I am in Paris in winter. I decide to visit Herta. From behind a door, I am watching her make love to a girl, a tough looking dyke I've seen at the Dôme. Her naked body gleams. Then Herta comes out. She has gotten fat and is not glad to see me.

This morning, I went to shit in my spot on the hill near the ruins of Sade's château. (We have no plumbing.) It is lovely there; the damp, rich earth.

I watched a tiny, mother-of-pearl snail, head and horns displayed, enjoying the weather.

Yesterday, at the market in Cavaillon, I saw a big, blonde gypsy woman with a bandana on her head and gold hoop earrings. She carried a baby on her hip in the same outfit. She was young and fierce looking, what pride of bearing!

AUGUST 19

I am sitting on the thorny hill looking down into the quarry. I am rereading, *Une saison en enfer* and really understanding it, at last. How had I not realized that *la vierge folle* was Verlaine and the *démon époux* Rimbaud? And how cruel he was, laughing at his love, at his ignorance, which made him the "foolish virgin." Was Rimbaud Verlaine's first homosexual love?

I wrote to Herta, "*Nous sommes deux vieilles tricotant dans le jardin d'un maison des fous . . . deux fillettes jouant a cache—cache entre les roues des camions . . .*"

She hated that letter and replied, sarcastically, "*Merci pour ta lettre charmante.*"

Sven works peacefully on the house. He is happy.

AUGUST 20

We went back to visit Lucien Jacques at Monjustin. There are photos on the wall of him with André Gide . . . Gide with his long, noble face, Jacques, young and hopeful.

Lucien's painting, *Le tombeau du berger* is a memorial to his lover. He said there were no photos of him, so he painted him on his deathbed. He said, "*Les photos sont une cimetière.*"

On the back of the motorcycle this afternoon, I kept thinking of my mother, picturing moments in her life—her first night with my father, whom she adored, the abortion she had later. She would have hugged my sister and me passionately before she left for the appointment. She would have wept. Of course, we couldn't understand. Much later, she told: "You would have had a little brother." Her guilt never left her. "It was a sin."

AUGUST 23
LACOSTE

On our kitchen wall there is a little painting, a seascape, that came with the house. A sailboat rushes silently through the dark, green, silent waves. There is a halo around the moon.

A poem:

> Scarecrow sweeps the days away,
>   but black wings cover her
> Pecked eyeless by the sun
> she waves a drowning hand to me,
> the flying sailor stranded here
>   on dusty tides of grass
> The log lies open on the mountain top.
> Its last words: the sea dries up.
> I saw gulls as black as nuns last night.
> We sink into the sand. What will
> the mermaids do when men
> walk their chambers and plant
> their roots in coral banks?
> Clover covers the anchor, drowned in dust.

SUNDAY, AUGUST 24

I woke up this morning saying, "This is our first summer without a cat." Later, a little one came to us. We call her "Sunday." She is black and white, with long whiskers and fleas. She sits in the sunny patch at the door.

Summer is almost over. Will we get back to Spain? I know I will have to go to my mother. I am already feeling nostalgic for what I am about to leave. At night, lying next to Sven, there is great sadness . . .

Notebook Three

My mother has had another operation on her face. Is it death walking toward her in those worn cheeks, those rough cheeks? I went down on my knees and prayed for her, with my hands over my face and tears running through my fingers, as I have seen her do over the Shabbos candles.

I had a letter today from Nanna. She advises me to leave Sven. (He read it this morning.) She had seen Herta in Munich and liked her. They had agreed in general that two women cannot make each other happy. Nanna has gone back to her old lover, Michael, who robbed her, and she is having her first exhibition of paintings.

Feeling a flood of fear. Sven was upset at the letter and just now, I am loving him again.

The new blue notebook, with its silky pages, is already holding a load of fear and sorrow.

SEPTEMBER 4

The sad angel of sickness still hovers over me. My cunt (I like to call it this to keep it in its place) still seems infected, the Bartholin gland still swollen. Sven is so gentle, delicate, almost motherly. *Le pauvre!* What happiness I may have given him was always ambivalent, bred from my troubled heart, my recalcitrant body, with its sudden spurts of sensuality. He reminded me yesterday that three years ago I had said I didn't want to see him again, that we had "nothing in common." It was our second meeting. But he persisted. Rimbaud says, "*D'ailleurs, je ne me le figurais pas avec une autre âme: on voit son Ange, jamais l'Ange d'un autre . . .*" Furthermore, I never imagined myself with another soul, one sees his own Angel, never the Angel of another . . . It is Verlaine, the "foolish virgin" speaking. Why don't I get well?

SUNDAY, SEPTEMBER 5

A long, quiet, melancholy day. Sven and I are at odds from waking. I am worried about this damn gonorrhea coming back and deeply regretting Spain. He is sad and quiet. He kindly looked in the cellar for a writing desk for me and came up with a strange little iron table on a wooden base, like sculptors use. My typewriter fits perfectly atop, looking handsome, like an object in a gallery.

Now Sven has gone off on the motorcycle, having invited me along, but I really didn't want to go. I am sitting in the sun, watching Sunday our little cat, at play. She leaps boldly into the small almond tree, climbing impetuously until, in a sudden panic, she drops rather clumsily to the ground. She makes tiny, intense sounds, and is more vocal than any other cat I've had.

SEPTEMBER 9

I would like to write an adventure story, a real one. It would begin something like this: "In Naples or Barcelona or Marseilles you are sure of your quarter. New York is another matter . . ."

SEPTEMBER 14

Herta may be coming this weekend. Heigh-ho, the wind and the rain!

But since learning of my mother's illness, the probable trip to New York, and the operation I will most likely need to have, I can't really concern myself with her. And something about her, something creepy and perverse in her letters has begun to disgust me. I think I want to be free of her.

This morning, I got a shattering letter from my mother. She is becoming more specific about her disease, feeling that I will eventually have to know the worst . . . cancer! She suggests that I might bring Sven with me, or have him join me in the States. And of course, I am carrying with me the jolly gift of the surgery that I myself will need to have, the removal of the Bartholin gland.

SEPTEMBER 27, 1953

I am going to Apt tomorrow for the operation, and I am glad. It was a sudden, inspired decision, and all the externals seem to support it—the wonderful doctor, the small fee arrangements—all of it! I am so tired of this anxiety, and I dread going to the States having still to deal with it.

I'll probably be in the hospital for a week with the nuns, in their black, translucent winged bonnets, taking care of me. Such pale, waxen faces they have; skin like paper, beaten and bleached. I shall speak French in my pain, a curious experience. Will it confirm my theory about the lightness of life in a foreign language?

SEPTEMBER 30, IN HOSPITAL
APT, FRANCE

The operation, a strangely sexual nightmare, is over, and today is my third day here. My pussy is shaved and stained with iodine, some blood still, an unpleasant odor. Being in hospital is almost enjoyable, peaceful, a sort of limbo. Outside my window, there is a little patch of countryside. Dogs walk by; old men lounge in the shade against stone walls. In this room, there are red, pink, and orange zinnias and a big bunch of sweet-smelling lavender brought by Sven.

OCTOBER 2, STILL IN HOSPITAL

I've spent this long, warm autumn day reading, dozing, eating . . . how lazy I am. I lack the energy even, to note down my thoughts about the book I'm reading, Georges Bernanos's *La joie.*

The sturdy nun with the hairy mole on her chin who washed me this morning is the one who shaved and strapped me down on the operating table. She is very masculine, robust, and competent. It was strange to see the gold wedding ring on her finger as she sponged my face. Bride of Christ, indeed!

How odd being in this Catholic environment, the plastic crucifix on my wall, the Bernanos novel, the manly, stout, gray-haired priest in black dress, whom I saw from my window just now, walking up the path to the pigpens. Fish for lunch because it's Friday. Strangely, I have so much more confidence in the sisters than in the lay attendants, who are probably no less intelligent and kind, but who lack the dedication one feels in the nuns.

Night . . .

My mother asks me to come home now, so we won't have that sweet time in Ibiza, my Sven and I, to keep as a charm over the absence.

MID-OCTOBER
IBIZA, SPAIN

We got here again, somehow, in spite of anxieties, but it is changed. There are too many foreigners here now, with their absurd scandals. Nevertheless, I hear the same songs in the street, the same women in black, calling, *"Hola, señora!"* glad to see me back. This time, we are staying in the Old Town. I love going down to the market through the lively streets, hearing the familiar sounds: dishes clattering, the chugging of fishing boats returning or departing, children laughing or weeping, the occasional thread of flamenco music, the loud bells telling time.

OCTOBER 22, SITTING ON THE ROCKS

I want this Ibiza to stay forever fresh in my memory, not to be confused with lovers, crises, departures. I want to keep it as it is in this moment: the sharp, foot-wounding rocks, the little islands I swim to, the tapping hammer sound from the dock, the bathtub splash below, and further out, the soft detonations of the waves, the wrinkled blue water with its patches of pink like birthmarks, the rosy cloud far off, and the nearby small hills. I want to hold this, this Ibiza.

NOVEMBER 3
BARCELONA

Goodbye, goodbye my sad darling. *Dors bien mon enfant. Buenas noches,* my love.

NOVEMBER 5
ABOARD THE *OLYMPIC*

My cabin mate is always sick, even when the boat is in harbor! When will she stop groaning?

It's hard to believe the Americans on this ship are real. They are such stereotypes!

Martha [Roberts, a photographer], the lesbian, reminds me of Peggy, with her pretensions, snobbery, and fetishes . . .cashmere sweaters, tweeds, her put-down of New York accents. They are not bad people, but so transparent. I much prefer the complicated Europeans . . .

NOVEMBER 8
AT SEA

I am popular on the ship, which surprises me. I am so used to being the odd one, alone.

Did I stay with Sven because I was afraid of always being that? Will my feelings toward him change with all these people approaching me?

NOVEMBER 10

Alone on the damp, windy deck watching a slim, curly-haired Italian sailor painting a mast. How beautiful he is! Fuck these sick, neurotic Americans, with their constant complaints!

NOVEMBER 12
HALIFAX

First sight of America. How ugly it looks!

NOVEMBER 14
NEW YORK

Back in the jungle, with its strange, striped, and spotted beasts, fierce or gentle; they roam wild in the streets. How pathetic I was, afraid for Martha to meet my family when we disembarked; the uncle who I said was "a friend of my mother's." How embarrassed I was to acknowledge my vulgar relatives! How ridiculous of me!

END OF NOVEMBER AT NEW YORK HOSPITAL

Here with my poor mother, mutilated by surgery. How she laughed and cried seeing me, seemed to gain strength from my presence. Half of her face is gone. To head off the cancer that was eating her away, the surgeons have removed most of her jaw. There is a hideous red hole where her cheek used to be. I force myself to watch as the nurse changes the dressing. Her feverish, anguished eyes bore into mine—pleading, "Look at me! No, don't look!"

Now my mother and I are staying at the old Beacon Hotel on upper Broadway, the neighborhood where I spent most of my childhood. We go daily to New York Hospital for her dressing change and radiation treatments. It is hard for her to talk, so we are mostly silent. She lies on one of the twin beds, watching television. Sometimes when I come back to the room, she is asleep, making that horrible gurgling sound as she breathes through her mouth, while the grainy, black-and-white TV drones on.

DECEMBER 2

Out with the "girls" to the dyke bars, like the *Bagatelle.* I realize, they don't interest me. How boring they are: Martha S. and her girlfriend Pat, Martha R., with her odd grimaces and profound and obvious fears. What really got to me was the way she reacted to the poor old drunk who asked for help crossing the street. And her annoying worship of superficial "chic" like the Plaza Hotel, Bergdorf's . . .

DECEMBER 8

Two nights ago, I visited an old high school friend, Barbara [Bank]. She is plump, rather dowdy, a recent Barnard graduate, an intellectual working in publishing and living in her first, very own apartment.

She had another guest, Maria Irene Fornes, a Cuban with an adorable Latina body, a round child's face, and a charming accent. We ate, drank a lot of wine, talked about Paris, careers, my mother . . .It got late, and Barbara invited me to sleep over on the couch. It was great to have a night away from that overheated hotel room, the sound of my mother's clotted breathing.

In the morning, Barbara left for work, and I stayed sleeping on the couch in that heavenly quiet. But suddenly, I was awakened by a warm, soft body, full breasts pressing against my back, a silky arm around my waist. Irene, the little Cubana, was under the blanket with me, drowning me in a passionate embrace. It was the beginning.

DECEMBER 14

Last night, we sang in bed while a heavy rain crashed outside. A mask she'd made grimaced on the wall. The world was very far away.

Then I got up and went back to the hotel, to my tragic mother waiting for me, sleepless. I feel now as if I am carrying two people on my shoulders . . .my mother and her. I don't know if I am strong enough for both.

DECEMBER 15

Writing a poem about her, in French, of course.

"Ah, belle Cubaine, qu'est ce que tu veux de moi?"

And so on.

Interruption, the telephone; it's *her.*

I am remembering Barcelona at night, the sex shops, the smell of *churros*, the sounds of clapping and heel-stamping from the gypsy nightclubs. The beautiful dancer, tall and robust, with dark skin, bright teeth, strong, sinuous hands. Sven and I ran into her at the public baths. I felt proud that she should see us doing such a non-touristy thing, taking a shower with *mi hombre* . . .

CHRISTMAS EVE
MIAMI, FLORIDA

Irene was here. We spent a whole day together, away from the New York intrigues. Joyous. Lying on the sand, swimming together. She slept in my arms last night. It was like a dream, after those New York goodbyes.

NEW YEAR'S EVE, 1954
MIAMI

What strange year is this, that comes to me in the tropics on a night of Cuban music, with the horror of tomorrow's job at the M&M cafeteria and the two letters that came today?

Sven is making plans full of hope, of solutions to our problems. *She* invites me, simply, to visit her in Cuba, without plans, only the powerful desire we feel for each other. How ironic it would be for me to abandon Sven just when he is finally establishing himself in Paris with a house, money, everything necessary to give me a home there, where I feel truly at home.

How to have my cake and eat it too? It can't be done. Only let me be with her for a while longer. Such beautiful nights and languorous mornings . . . what delight she gives me!

JANUARY 1, 1954
MIAMI, AFTER MIDNIGHT

I smoke this year's first cigarette but don't shed this year's first tear; I know I will need it later.

JANUARY 6

I am sick in bed with intestinal flu, the inevitable result of my wretchedness here. To be feverish in a twin bed in the dreary atmosphere of my childhood. Yesterday, when my fever was higher, I read my sister's TB sanatorium journals. They are tragic. They made me cry. How strong she was. Only at the end, when her new life is beginning, is there weakness, the desire to escape herself. And now she has succeeded in stifling the deepest, tenderest voice of her soul. How good it was to recover that voice in her journals!

My diaries mean so much to me; though they preserve so little, this little is precious. Bobbie said disapprovingly, "Writers all care so much about history."

JANUARY 8

Mother is back in New York. She is terribly sick. When I consider how tortured I have been lately about love, Sven, decisions, and then see how death decides it all, it seems foolish. Will I be able to abandon her struggle? How long will the battle be, and must I stand by her until the end? I wish I could believe in God . . . unless he is just a spoiler, a prison guard! Fuck him if that's all he is!

JANUARY 19, 1954

She was here yesterday and the day before. Left this evening. Last night we danced together in a bar, and everyone could see our love. She wanted to stay another day, but I realized, suddenly, that my father *knew*! It made me think of that episode in Proust when Vinteuil's daughter makes love to her friend in front of a picture of her father. Dad phoned from downtown and said, "Get that girl out of the house!" He was furious! When I am with her, I am in another world without father, sister, mother. Miami is just a backdrop. For two whole days, we stayed in bed making love, only going out at night.

What can I do? I am trapped indefinitely in this family prison . . .

JANUARY 20

My situation here gets worse all the time. Dad asks embarrassing questions: "Do you miss masculine company?" meaning sex. He talks a lot about "yesterday." "When you were shut up in your room with the door locked, I couldn't get your attention." Sarcasm? When he called me, where were we? In the shower? He talks a lot about Sven, suggests that he should come here. And why don't you marry him? It's awful! Fingers seem to point at me from all sides: Sven, my family, and probably Barbara B. in New York. It makes me feel ugly and dirty.

FEBRUARY 7
AT WELLESLEY COLLEGE WITH SARAH BETSKY

Sunday afternoon, Monteverdi madrigals, clear winter skies, bicycles on the lawn. On Friday night, when I left to take the train, she said, "I'm afraid."

"Why?"

"Because you are going. . ."

FEBRUARY 8, SNOWING

Ask its name, this shy creature, finger to finger, creeping into your heart. Ah, little gray crab, dancer, back and side, guts and lungs, and even into the crowded brain. Ah, cancer!

FEBRUARY 14, VALENTINE'S DAY

Tonight, I wanted to go to the bar to show her off to Martha S. and her girlfriend Pat. But Pat came on to her, and she responded and would have gone farther if I had been blind. But I saw it and broke it up, and everything got ugly. The taste of vomit in my mouth, the taste of jealousy that Peggy taught me, reminds me of a hideous time in my life. Yes, it's like that, love between women. It has to be hidden, not just from the world, but because it is so fragile that a touch can destroy it.

My mother is dying. Everything, that is, Europe, seems farther and farther away. What will become of me in these months of ordeal? What will I be when it's over? Will I be glad when she dies?

MARCH 1

Warm, gray morning.
This is the first lesbian affair of my life that satisfies

me sexually, or even more, that is *truly* sexual. It's
odd, because she doesn't appear to be the kind of
woman to inspire grand passions, perhaps because
she is so simple and sane. However, she does seem to
want to make me suffer.

Today, again, I will ask my mother's doctor how
much time she has left. It is March, my birth month,
the month when Proserpine returns to earth.

MARCH 3, 1954, ASH WEDNESDAY

It's raining. Irene is all I care about, but it would be
insane to deliver my life into her little thief's hands,
her greedy, child's hands. . .

MARCH 7

These are terrible days knowing I won't be able to
leave. April first is so near, and her death is still so
far. I lead a schizophrenic life in the room at the Beacon Hotel. I sit like an idol, a mute, and move only
when she needs me. I sit in silence when the television torture is off, listening to her belching, retching,
moaning. . .the horrible sounds torn from her dying
body. I can't seem to find anything comforting to say
to give her strength.

And then, away from here, there are evenings like at the party last night when I felt strong

and beautiful and danced and was admired and desired. Another world! I am suspended between two extremes: misery and joy.

MARCH 14

Early yesterday morning, Barbara B. phoned to tell me that Irene's place had been broken into and she was missing and did I know where she was. Later, she returned to the apartment with two other people and called me, saying, "You better come down here. There's a lot of stuff of yours lying around. . ." . . . Little love notes, a silly pornographic photo, medical notes on gonorrhea for me and even for Sven. She was clearly excited by images of scandal and crimes of passion. I asked her to remove anything too personal and she refused, saying, "What would my friends think?" She so disgusted me, her fear of exposure and her willingness to expose me and Irene, whom she pretends to love. So I became afraid too, for that foolish creature who had kept all my tender and angry notes lying on her mantelpiece like precious objects.

Irene called at two in the afternoon. She knew nothing about her apartment. We went downtown together in the subway. What a relief to find her unharmed! I do love her. Last night, at Buddy's place, we lay on the bed reading *Babar* and then turned off the light and made hurried love, whispering, scared, and beautiful. . .

And guess what? The thieves stole my Levis!

MARCH 27, 1954

Yesterday was my 25th birthday, a sad day after a bad night with Mother. I went to work, and back at the hotel, there was underwear and a cake. Later, I went to Irene's. There were small gifts everywhere, prettily ribboned: a book of Spanish poetry, another of Lorca's, a record of Lola Flores's *Pena, Penita, Pena*, our favorite flamenco song, a doll she made for me, small and exquisite like herself, holding a tiny card and a miniscule rose.

Tonight we are in a motel in Montauk. She is in the shower, and the doll is on the table between the beds along with a deck of Tarot cards, another of her gifts to me. We were on the beach all afternoon—wind, pure sea air, the many-colored pebbles and shells.

What a wonderful day it has been! How wonderful she is, this great little girl with her Spanish sailor's walk, in those tight jeans that show off her round ass like a Hindu goddess's! Seagull in Spanish is *gaviota*. . .

APRIL 5

I am finally learning how to steer clear of pain. Example: the proposed weekend with Martha S. and her girlfriend. In the old days, I would have taken the dare, risked my joy with Irene. Why? To rid myself of her, to test her? I remember Peggy always putting me and herself in dangerous situations. And now it strikes me as a revelation that I don't *need* to take on Pat's challenge. Maybe I have gained a sort of maturity about love. To not be always seeking "the secure torment." [See *Nightwood*].

And, too, I am more at peace since I wrote to Sven. Being dishonest makes me feel ill. Maybe I didn't tell him everything. Maybe I never will. But at least I have let him know that I am involved in something else. I do believe in honesty. Honesty, to me, is freedom.

Barbara B.'s letter to us was silly and pathetic. She sees herself as the injured party, the martyr. She forgives us for causing her pain. But I don't forgive her for what she did at the time of the break-in, how she wouldn't protect me or even Irene, whom she professes to love. What a cowardly revenge!

April 26

In my new apartment, 61 Avenue A, a beautiful loft where all my fantasies settle in comfortably amid strange books, flowers, toys. . .

MAY 9

Sunday morning, *chez moi.* The sun is out but we stay in. Friday night I gave a party to show her off, my new treasure. Lots of old friends came. Some of them disapproved of her, dressed as she was in flounces, like a little tart. Others thought her adorable. Everyone could see that I am in love!

JUNE 8

A summer evening. I sit at my window looking out at the fern-like trees in the backyard, the two cats posed on the iron railings of the fire escape. A blue kite over the roof. As night falls, the neon sign of the cafeteria across the street begins to stain my windows red. I have a wonderful job with an antiquarian book dealer. I am loving New York!

Soon I return to Paris. Will I ever be able to write about these months? So much that is lovely and tragic has happened. My guilt toward my mother, my love for Irene..

JULY 1
MIAMI

Daddy's profound cowardice shows in everything he does. His response to mother's condition is to behave negatively. . .to *unbehave* toward her. He never looks directly at her; he never speaks directly to her. The moment he is alone, he begins that horrible kvetching "O GOD!" sighing heavily. He dislikes me almost as much as he hates her, but he knows that I am stronger than he and that I don't love him the way she does. He nags me constantly in the car, criticizing my driving, which lacks his own dangerous caution. He bought an awful lamp "from the night manager at the Mayflower" for five dollars. He speaks warmly of the boy. How sad that he never had the son he so desired.

The old photographs he has had restored—a portrait of mother at age twenty, almost pretty, mounted on a mirror back, and a picture of him, aged thirty, *tres beau,* on a pin like a campaign button for Wilkie or FDR. Seeing her now with her mutilated face next to that smiling dark-haired young woman is horrible!

She tells me there should be eight thousand dollars for Bobbie and me from the sale of the store when she dies; cautions that we must not let ourselves be cheated should he take up with some designing woman. She turns increasingly toward death. Standing on the garden steps, she points, "See those flowers? They go to sleep at night. . ." In her hideousness, she looks everywhere for beauty. My heart aches.

JULY 6

I am reading the Bible to my mother. I leave tomorrow.

JULY 9,
PROVINCETOWN WITH IRENE

Talked to Mom on the phone. She had been crying.
Will I ever see her again? Words, words, they are so
empty, so banal. But what *can* one say? I lie. I say,
"Somebody is watching over you. . ." Yes, the great
God, the great blanket, the Great Blank. . .

JULY 16
ON THE BOSTON BOAT

Waving goodbye to one more person I love, from
the deck of this, a small model of the boat I shall
be boarding next Tuesday. I dread reading the letter
from Paris that must be waiting for me in New York.
My mother is dying. I move from scene to scene.
Why do I never meet happiness?

JULY 19

I sail tomorrow. Irene showed up last night from P-
town and we said goodbye again. I wish she hadn't

come. The farewell at the Boston boat was so much sweeter than this morning's hasty love-making and subway adieux. It may have been a mistake, but oh, the inexpressible joy I felt when, calling down the stairs, I heard her little voice: "It's Irene. . ."

JULY 21
ABOARD THE LIBERTÉ

I feel light and free. What use is there in worrying about the future? I guess I'll just leave it up to Sven.

JULY 22

Reading George Sand: "If I had found a man capable of dominating me, I should have been saved, for liberty is eating my life away and killing me."

Just finished *Two Serious Ladies* by Jane Bowles. It's about a nice little wife whose "poet" husband drags her to exotic places where she, by accident, discovers her true nature when she falls in love with the Spanish prostitute. Of course, she was married to Paul Bowles and lived with a Moroccan woman. Resonates with me.

JULY 25

Tomorrow, Paris. Irene, bab, I would love to be in bed with you now, sucking on your beautiful breast while you stroke my hair. The love I refused my mother, I have given to you.

Paris, how it was: I got off the train at the *gare St. Lazare* after six days on the ship. It was nine in the evening, a spring evening—opal roses lingered in the sky. The air around the station smelled of chestnut blossoms and car exhaust. Noisy people rushed by, swept along on the evening tide. A tall, serious-looking man came toward me, and I entered his embracing arms. "Sven! How wonderful to see you!" I smelled the faint, tobacco-tainted scent of his body as I nuzzled my face into his chest. We crossed the boulevard to a café table. "What would you like, darling?" he asked softly.

"Pernod," I replied. I needed a powerful hit of alcohol to ease my way into what was bound to be a difficult conversation. We talked. He told me about his new place, his work, how much he had missed me. I had a second Pernod. We took a cab home, undressed hurriedly, and made love. . . . And I felt *nothing*.

We both began to weep. Then I told him. "I'm in love with someone else. . .a woman."

JULY 30, 1954
15 RUE DE LA HARPE, PARIS

I am settled into my own little room, with all my books, toys, mementos. Sven is in his house, far from the *quartier*. Mother is far away in Miami, in her house, dying. I don't seem to feel his sadness, nor hers. Is my heart dead? If it is, why do I feel this hidden pleasure? Is it freedom, or just the satisfaction of having brought Sven to tears?

AUGUST 1

Everyone here says I have changed, gotten "hard". Sven, Sydney, Herta, and Pierre Humbert (that dirty little yellow-faced *vicieux*). They say "Americanized." I had been accepting their version of things until this moment, when I realized that these people have only known me as "Sven's girl." Even Sven's idea of me has never been very exact. Have I really changed? Something *has* happened to me, thanks to my mother and Irene. I have learned that loving is selfish; being loved, unselfish.

I'm more interested in sex than I've been in years. I feel as I did when I was thirteen, fearful and enthralled. And I now realize that I never liked Sven in bed. It has taken me a while to recognize that. I was not excited by his body, his mouth, his smell, etc.

What confused me was that he made love so well (orally) which is, clearly, just one part of the picture.

AUGUST 4

I have two flamenco records and *Pena Penita* by Lola Flores, my favorite. Sven is wretched. He still doesn't get what I want, which is for us to be friends who sleep together occasionally. I feel closest to him when we are alone, but annoyed with him in public.

I listen to the flamenco records and feel I am in Spain. I listen to *Pena* and know I am in love.

AUGUST 13

Still no word from Irene. It's raining, and Paris is cold and gray. I like summer to be hot, not like this. Lucky for the Parisians, there are Arabs and Africans here who carry heat and laughter into the streets. Otherwise they would be even paler.

AUGUST 16

Sven is really strange. He rebels against all the good things in life: comfort, cleanliness, fine food. He is a masochistic lover as well. And something else I have just realized . . . his penis is *too small* for me! This is probably why I never enjoyed intercourse with him. I can hardly feel it!

Tomorrow I am hitchhiking to St.-Tropez. I need to get away from dark Paris, and waiting. . .

AUGUST 18
MARSEILLE

How much more exciting and dangerous it is without Sven. Went to Avignon this morning. . .peacocks in the garden. I vaguely remember arguing with him about the differences between males and females. When I saw the splendid blue husband with his small brown wife, I felt triumphant.

I think a lot about Irene. One of the girls I am traveling with reminds me of her, but is so much less vibrant. All I am really doing is *waiting* for her.

AUGUST 21
ST.-TROPEZ, *CHEZ* SAM WOLFENSTEIN

There is an awful atmosphere here. I used to like Sam, but since his marriage he has changed. There is something mean and petty about him. He's become terribly stingy with money; afraid of wasting it on pleasure; worried about being repaid for things. And he imposes these feelings on his wife.

St.-Tropez is very much like Provincetown, lots of pretty girls and lesbians. I sense a growing reckless-ness in myself; not good. Whatever foolishness I may commit now it's always with the *arriere pensee* (hid-den motive) of hurting Irene. But of course, as Proust points out, when you are no longer loved, nothing you do matters to the one you love.

I feel strongly that I should stay here as long as I can to postpone the misery of waiting in Paris.

AUGUST 22
ST.-TROPEZ

The Mistral. Rain blowing around. This afternoon on the nude beach—so many beautiful women!

AUGUST 28
LYONS, HITCHHIKING

I'm in a windowless hotel room on my way back to Paris. I got a ride today from a Chinese man in a fast German car. He invited me to spend the night with him here, a strange, calm, "inscrutable" fellow. I couldn't figure him out. Will he take me the rest of the way to Paris as he promised, even though I turned him down?

As I walked back to this dismal room tonight, a little, clerkish man said to me, *"Il fait plaisir de vous voir, Mlle. Vous respirez le soleil!"* (It's a treat to see you miss. You smell of the sun!)

In this gray city, I look brown and wild in my new sandals, with the chamois bag that Mim made for me in Black Mountain. My mother said in her last letter that I should always be by the sea in the sun; it makes me beautiful.

AUGUST 30
PARIS

Irene is coming soon. I spent the evening with Herta, walking the quays. I don't think we will ever sleep together. My mother is dying, and I am no longer a child.

SEPTEMBER 1

I am trying to write while the noises from the street come tramping through my head.

Motorcycles bore through like hot corkscrews. (Cockscrews?) Am I really as perverse as they say? Am I a poisoner? Irene seems to think so. She writes, "I see how tremendously bitter I am towards you. I guess it is a bitterness I felt before, too, but your presence made me forget about it more."

In the park behind the church of *Saint-Julien-le-Pauvre.*

What a lovely, bright autumn morning! Notre Dame shines across the river. Children play quietly—so French! It's much more peaceful here than in my room. Two Spanish ladies chat behind me.

I am my mother's life, but she is not mine. So sad. I *am* her life, just as Peggy, Sven, Irene, the children I will have, are mine.

SEPTEMBER 2

From *Querelle de Brest* by Jean Genet

> *Deux frères qui s'aiment jusqu'à se ressembler . . .*
> *Deux frères qui se ressemblent jusqu'à s'aimer . . .*

(Two brothers who love each other so much they look alike. Two brothers who look so much alike they love each other.)

Now why don't I write her? Revenge? I won't write until three days before she sails, so she'll have time to think about things.

SEPTEMBER 8

As for the "count" who gave me a ride to Paris in August, he asked me to become his mistress, his "back street" like the old movie with Margaret Sullavan. Sven's reaction when I told him about it was disgusting. "You should have accepted it," he said. He only took it back after I told him how offended I was and that it showed how little he understands me. As for the Count, I just remembered something he said in the car. He called me "*ma petite Harriet*" and I replied, "*Je ne suis pas ta petite Harriet. Je suis ma grande Harriet!*" He thought for a moment and said, rubbing his head against my shoulder, "*Alors, si tu es la tienne, prends-moi aussi. . .*" I thought that was very sweet, and it's pretty obvious that a man who wants a woman twice his height must be masochistic and effeminate. He spoke of his powerful mother and his late marriage and signed his note to me "*Votre chauffeur.*"

However, his masculine side appeared when he bragged about his estates, businesses, etc. At the same time, leaning against me, he said, "*Comme c'est bien de rester la tête sur ton epaule. . .*" I replied, "*Tu es un petit chat. . .*"

Now we are each waiting for the other's next move. I will not pursue him; it would be too silly, not my kind of life at all.

Back to work at Fauchon, the elite gourmet market, tomorrow.

SEPTEMBER 23

Mother is dying and I must go to her.

Last night I slept with Nissan [Rilov], an Israeli painter. He is attractive with a strong, bony, Christ-like body and a beautiful rugged face, but he couldn't make it. I think I confused him. I was terrified that he would say he'd heard I was a lesbian. I must be careful not to let things go the way they did in New York. I still do love men!

Irene arrives tomorrow night and I am nervous about meeting her at the *gare St.-Lazare*. And then what? My mother is dying. . .

SEPTEMBER 28

Irene is here. I do love her, but it is increasingly clear that she is no longer in love with me.

SEPTEMBER 29

I spent last night with George, drowning our sorrows. Odd how surprised I was to hear him mention "this guy" who is making me unhappy. I've gotten so used to homosexuality that most people's natural assumption of my lover's gender seems strange to me.

Nissan asked me to live with him!

Yom Kippur.

Mother, Mother!

OCTOBER 20
MADRID, WITH IRENE

Our distance from each other grows greater every day. She disappears suddenly, goes to sleep, or just sits there with her eyes open, blank as a mirror. . .

OCTOBER 21

We took a happy walk in the sun this morning, passing a train station called *Mediodia*, a modern tile-and-glass cathedral surrounded by pines. On the roof, huge iron letters say, Madrid, Valencia, Alicante.

Went to a bullfight this afternoon. As always, there were moments of beauty: the *banderillero* in pink, strutting forward on tiptoes; a young matador advancing on the bull with the *muleta* slung over his hip like an evening cloak, his swaying buttocks. Another boy was gored, tossed into the air over the bull's head, while the crowd screamed for blood.

Last night we went to a theater to hear Lola Flores. The place was terribly hot, and when we went to the lobby at intermission, the men stared rudely at us smoking. I don't like Madrid; it is a big, dull place, nothing like Barcelona.

We go to Málaga tomorrow.

November 10
On the Train to Madrid

Irene is staying in Málaga. She looked adorable at the station in her furry brown "monkey" jacket, her little tanned hand waving.

How small her mouth is. "Do you like small lips?" Last night she dreamed I was making love to her and suddenly stopped. "Jesus Christ!" she screamed and I replied, "Do you always have to have an orgasm?" She woke up. Later in the morning, when we awoke again, I made love to her. Her closed eyes, half-smiling mouth, little white teeth: How happy she looked!

Afterward she said, "That was better than in the dream."

"Stay, stay," she said, and then, "I don't know if I really want you to." I feel the same ambivalence about her coming back to Paris.

The other night, we went out with two Spanish guys. She left early, and when I got back to the hotel, she was already in bed, acting strange. The next day, she said, "I thought you were going to screw that guy!" It was great to see her jealous!

In this compartment with me are the following: an army officer so stupid he can't even close the window (thank God), a couple with a screaming baby, and an old man with white hair and a big nose who belches like a pig. His wife and daughter are here too, with an enormous bag full of food. I have one *chirimoya*, a tough-skinned green fruit with a creamy white inside, juicy and sweet like a pineapple-banana, four fat bananas, and three oranges with stems and leaves still attached.

I wish this fucking baby would shut up!

MONDAY, 1:30 P.M.
MADRID

Sitting at a café, so tired, in a daze. The train to Paris is at ten o'clock tonight. How will I get through this day?

5:00 P.M.
MADRID

Just left the Prado, where I visited the Flemish collection. Such sexy experiments going on in Bosch's *Garden of Delights*! The day moves along smoothly.

TUESDAY, ON THE TRAIN

Will my room be warm? Who will be around to greet me? It is cold and rainy, while she is on the Costa Brava in the sun. When will they call me from New York? When I try to picture my mother, all I can see is that hideous wet bubble of flesh in her face and her desperate eyes. . .

Two very loud and drunk trainmen come into the compartment and stare at me. The old lady keeps knitting, occasionally smiling, sympathetically, in my direction. The good-looking young paratrooper with ice-blue eyes has gone into the corridor, leaving his book on the seat opposite me, which had been empty. I think it was so he could be there to protect me from the drunks—or maybe he just dropped it by mistake.

NOVEMBER 14
PARIS

I begin to remember loneliness. Also, my sexual appetite is so much stronger now than it used to be. Imagine, it's been only a week since I made love with Irene, and already I am starving. When Sven was here the other day, I wanted him, but he pretended not to notice. Tonight I was planning to sleep with Nissan, but then, all that hanging around in cafés and Jacob's presence annoyed me, and I decided to leave. He didn't try to stop me.

Soon I will be in the States where there will be only hunger, mourning, and pain.

NOVEMBER 19, 1954

About to reenter that stupefying world of transatlantic crossings on my way back to New York—to my mother's death, my father's collapse, my sister's estrangement from me. Irene, where are you? After that one desperate letter, there's been no news at all. Will she suffer when she returns to Paris and finds me gone?

At the station, Sven kissed me hard, a frightened look on his face. Sam and Hannes came with a book and a bottle of wine; Kenneth Koch with ambiguous jokes. Two nights ago, I met Han [van der Ploeg], a tall, silver-haired Dutch boy with a strong, catlike face, beautiful and intense. He came up to my room and we smoked cigarettes and talked. I would gladly have slept with him, but these northerners are not like the French or the Italians. They take sex much more seriously.

In Nissan's studio, deeply asleep, he bent over and kissed me goodbye, saying he hoped to see me when I return. *Oh Pupi, donde estas? Que te pasa?* I ask this in Spanish so you might hear it better.

NOVEMBER 20
ABOARD THE *ILE-DE-FRANCE*

A winter sea, pink in the west; the sailors painting the deck, dressed in blue-green denims, silhouetted against the sky.

My hands are cold. Already feeling the bleak, hypochondriacal, morbid influence of New York. Thinking of Han.

NOVEMBER 21

Rough weather. I am determined not to be seasick. This is the worst crossing I've made, with awful people at my table in the dining room and awful women in my cabin.

Last winter is about to begin again—the daily visits to the hospital, the dark streets, watching the destruction of my poor mother's body and spirit. I keep wanting to say to her "Mom, you must go now; you must rest . . . " I want her to escape from the hell into which this disease has plunged her . . . the pain . . . .

SUNDAY NIGHT
NEW YORK

My mother has become a hideous, shrunken child. But I remember her as she was, the strong, bossy, energetic woman who made all the decisions in our family. How powerful she was then, this poor, baffled creature, all skin and bones. My sadness is somehow made bearable by the feeling that I am in the right place, fulfilling my duties, being a good daughter. I love her more now than I ever did before.

MONDAY
NEW YORK

What is all this nastiness, the cold blue eyes of the desk clerk, the sullen pout of the black bus driver? I waited endlessly in the slick Doubleday offices until the pock-marked, bitter-looking secretary, staring at me as if I were from another planet, told me "No job." I guess I just don't match up with their idea of an editorial assistant.

They say my mother will be gone soon.

DECEMBER 12, 1954
NEW YORK

MOTHER DIED TODAY.
To Remember: I sat at her bedside watching her struggle to breathe, knowing the struggle would soon be over. She opened her tormented eyes to me, and, wanting to comfort her, I said, "Mom, you know the Israeli guy I told you about? I might marry him." "No, you won't," she whispered. "Why not, Mom?" I asked, surprised. "Because, because," she struggled

to bring it out, "because you like women better," and her eyes closed on a deep, strangled sigh. Those were her last words to me. She went into the dark with that sad thought.

A small black tear tolled down her cheek. How quickly death took her; how quickly she went from sleep to forever! She is gone, she is gone, only fifty-three! Now she is all alone in the hospital room, and they have covered her poor, mutilated face and closed her suffering eyes. Oh, Mom, how I will miss your terrible presence!

DECEMBER 19
IN MY SISTER'S HELL'S KITCHEN LOFT

It is Sunday, 1:00 p.m. Bobbie is asleep in her room with her lover, Brendan. And a big, beautiful, muscular boy named Peter sleeps in my bed. I have finally found out what a really good fuck should be. . .yes, size is all important! He is nineteen and big in every way, sweet but dumb, but so what? I keep thinking of the Dietrich song, "Peter," where she says, "*war mein beste stucke*," and he sure is mine! How odd that I should finally get it right after my mother's death.

And what about Irene?

DECEMBER 26, 1954

The unthinkable has happened—Irene writes that she is in love with a man, Diorka, Herta's ex-lover. I have been drinking since I got her letter on Friday. Today is Sunday. Thank God I am here, far away, and don't have to witness it, can turn it off like a radio program. And then, of course, there's Peter!

What a momentous December this has been, Mother and Irene both leaving me.

On Christmas Eve I went to church with Helen de Mott and lit a candle for Mom. Later, I went to bed with Peter and had the great comfort of these amazing orgasms! What a revelation!

JANUARY 8, 1955

As of yesterday, I am also sleeping with Harry Bell. How different he is from Peter. . .thin, tense, poetic. Our kisses are his pleas for strength. Peter is big and strong and dumb. He makes me his puppet, and I love it. But I like making it with Harry too. . .the smell of the *Celtiques* he smokes, the scar where his leg was broken, his slim, hairless body. His face is beautiful too. . .high cheekbones, long, serious nose, soft, pleading blue eyes. He resembles Jean-Louis Barrault. When he left to go home to his pregnant wife, I lay contentedly in bed, listening to Bartók.

Being with him feels like Paris.

Harry in the afternoon, Peter at night. . .heaven!

JANUARY 12

Today I got another fantastic letter from Irene. We are like lion and tamer—taking turns at each role. She writes, "I'm just a fucking lesbian, baby," regarding why things didn't work out with Diorka. She says she won't take "no shit" from a man that I gave her a worse time than he did, but she put up with it because I am a woman. She asks if I'm getting something *new* from Peter and Harry, sexually. Obviously she's concerned about this.

JANUARY 14

A love letter from Irene full of scenes from our life together: "blowing my nose into the wind on the beach with you," "in the car with you in Miami," "you are the only person I could ever sleep with while embracing all night long."

Harry came over tonight; the fourth time we've made it. He is a deeply troubled guy. And what can I do for him? Keep on giving, like Mother Earth. He called me "mother night" in his poem. He feels so guilty and inadequate. Thinks his penis is too short, while I find it quite satisfactory. His neurosis may do what our pleasure has not. . .expose us!

JANUARY 16—THIS INTERMINABLE MONTH!

There are floods in Paris! The Seine climbing up onto the quays. How I'd love to see it! Had another letter from Irene: "I want you." Will she still feel that way when I return?

Here, it is a warm, sunny winter. I am enjoying my snug routine: five days of work at Lathrop C. Harper, the rare book dealer, weekends with Peter and Harry, and occasionally The Bagatelle [dyke bar].

JANUARY 25

Here I am in Hell's Kitchen, smoking a cigarette, listening to the liners groaning and moaning on the Hudson. I had dinner alone, read Cocteau's *Opium*. It's very intelligent, often brilliant, but not in the least poetic.

When I got in from work both Harry and Peter phoned. Peter is becoming impossible! He is so damned stupid and loves to talk. If only he would just fuck me with that gorgeous dick and not expect me to hold a conversation with him!

Sudden twinge of fear; is Mother here? How

quickly the dead are dead, and yet, as I write this, I do not really believe that she is gone.

The ships cry.

FEBRUARY 2

I sail in twenty-three days. I am finally getting bored with this empty sex. I want to be pure.

FEBRUARY 25, ABOARD THE *MAASDAM*

Another ship! I leave New York, this time with affection: Harry who loves me, Peter who gave me joy and will soon forget me, my sister Bobbie, and my mother in the wet spring earth. I don't even know the name of the cemetery. But she is still with me.

At the moment, I am sitting on deck watching a Dutch sailor at work, his shirt and pants flapping in the wind. I am loving this whole week of relaxing in the warm, salty breeze, admiring the adolescent sailors, with their long hair, their flat white hats worn low on the forehead with ribbon streamers flying behind. . .

FEBRUARY 26, ABOARD THE *MAASDAM*

Cliff, the young Englishman with the green eyes and handsome, fanatical face, has taken over the confused effeminate American and moved into his cabin. Will the poor thing stick to his marriage plans?

MARCH 1

Fine, busy weather, lots of motion; dishes sliding back and forth on the tables. This is the heart of the voyage, when you know enough people to play games with and are close enough to the end for sensible withdrawal. Last night I got drunk with the Dutch painter who said the following to me: "*À l'âge de douze ans j'avais lu tout Dostoevsky et je t'aimais déjà mais je n'ai jamais su te plaire. . .*" I have no idea what he meant, but it was flattering to be identified with a heroine in Dostoevski. And he was right; his weakness, his pretentiousness could never please me.

This is a good ship.

MARCH 9
PARIS, *HÔTEL NOTRE-DAME*

The Seine runs right below my window. I sit and watch its silky density, whirlpools of light, and the *place de Notre-Dame* across the way, lit by three-branched lamps—bright, empty, sinister and beautiful. Paris is sinister and beautiful too. . .

MARCH 15

I tried to write about Mother's funeral today but just couldn't.

MARCH 27, 1955

My twenty-sixth birthday, the second spent with Irene. I got my period and felt lousy, but she held me in her arms and made it better. She bought me the African earrings. In the evening, I looked out the window and there was Martin on the quay. I called out to him. He seems taller and wider, more manly.

Last night at the Café Royale for my birthday celebration. At first, it was just us, me and Irene, but then Paul and Marion and Han with his little French wife showed up. Herta brought me flowers. Irene was an angel.

APRIL 1

Tonight, I remembered going to the movie, *Mogambo in Miami*, and Mother driving to the theater to pick me up, sick as she was, with her bandaged face, wrapped in an old bathrobe. She was so happy that night, happy to be alone with me, to be driving, to feel free! Those drives we took, just the two of us at night, roaring along the dark highways. When I parked at the beach that time, she got frightened and thought I would roll into the ocean, I got angry at her. Oh, darling, how many times did you tell me, "You'll be sorry some day for being mean to me now? . . ."Yes, Mom, I am sorry for my cruelties to you."

END OF APRIL
LUXEMBOURG GARDENS

It is hot, and the grass is studded with tiny white flowers. No wind. Only one lonely little sailboat in the basin; a small boy leading it around the rim with a stick.

Now, Irene tells me we are seeing too much of each other, which keeps her from "other things," "other people." I really wanted to hit her, but all I did was to slam the door. I suddenly remember a passage from *Nightwood*: "the same dog will . . . " dig up Nora's and Robin's bones. Peggy was my Robin.

MAY 1

A night of drunkenness. I went to her at daybreak. She smiled. I slept. She made breakfast for me in bed and then, weeping, talk, talk, talk. She said, "I must have lovers and admirers, or I feel like I'm dead." We both wept.

I love you, Irene. How well you fill my need for pain!

MAY 3

Why doesn't Sven come to see me? I am very hot for a man. . .

MAY 8

Sven. Tall, calm, very thin, with an unappetizing mustache. Fatherly and affectionate. How nasty of me to have wanted sex to make him miss me more. He is very careful not to arouse my jealousy of Romaine. I felt a slight regret on seeing photos from Lacoste. And he urges me to get back to writing.

MAY 12

Playing the mime game in the street tonight with Irene, Ricardo Vigón and Alejandro Jodorowsky. Each of us very clearly expressing our own needs and personality. Ricardo walks humbly up to us crying "Help!"; Irene plays the timid, flirtatious child; I, fearful and contemptuous at once, turn my back to them, take out a letter and read it, make them wait, and finally, give money to Irene. Alejandro understands. He runs toward us, a horribly affected ballet run, smiling, showing how pleased he is with himself!

MAY 15

Yesterday was Irene's birthday. I gave her a necklace of Venetian glass beads, blue, gold, and white. Tonight, she gave me the gift of confessing her affair with Herta! How I hate that filthy bitch, who betrayed me—sleeping with my love while pretending to care for me! I wish her dead!

MAY 16

I have fallen and been betrayed. I feel like the paralytic who rolls down Bd. St.-Germain on a plank with wheels. I have seen my mother's death. I am profoundly drunk with wine, with walking, with falling.

I sit in the little park of the Vert-Galant. It is warm and quiet and gray. A barge passes by and fills the silence with the happy sound of its pulsing engines. The grass is very green and crowded with monotonously chirping sparrows.

MAY 22
ON THE TRAIN TO MUNICH

After a ridiculous struggle to get this notebook out of my valise, I am ready to make note of the phony, refined old lady, the peasant woman, and the sluggish gentleman who finally helped me. I am reading Virginia Woolf's diary, which made me desperate to get to my own.

It's been a very strange week, starting last Sunday with Irene's confession about Herta. She keeps coming around, but I don't want to see her. She is very unhappy. I left her a note saying, "When I see you suffering, my heart tears apart like a handkerchief."

On my way to the movie *Brief Encounter,* I ran into her. She was happy to see me. After the movie, still raining, I went to the Bonaparte. That blonde fake *lesbienne*, Hillary, asked me to go with her to the Monocle [dyke bar], where we danced. Hillary had to go home, and we stopped on the way for a drink in the *rue de Buci.* An Irishman came along, she left and I ended up in bed with him in his strange, old, plushy room. Some kind of sex.

Next day, Irene came. She was upset when I told her I'd had an orgasm with the Irishman. In a flash of real jealousy, she called me a "whore." That night I saw Luce Klein, an old acquaintance from Berkeley. Then I met Sven and Romaine, with Han and his wife Monique. Romaine, being provocative as always her pale, beautiful face, her ugly hair and coat. I guess I should have gone to Lacoste with them when they invited me. Sven is looking tired, old and poor. Han, handsome and friendly, perhaps a bit resentful of my criticism of his English pronunciation.

Later, I dropped into the Mabilion and found Irene with Alejandro. He was very friendly, and Irene showed some jealousy. She and I went home together.

On Thursday, we got up late and made love all afternoon. On Friday, we went to Amex for mail and ran into Elliot Stein. I had a letter from Harry. Her jolly mood vanished and she left.

It's always the same old thing: she tells me I "limit" her, and I tell her I'm bored with her complaints.

We have just passed a town called Lunevile. A peculiar, ugly girl, with thick glasses and magnified eyes, is staring at me.

MAY 25 MUNICH

I am having a fine time here with Nanna, who is stronger than ever, powerfully sane, in good shape. She says I have lost that marvelous "hardness" I used to have, that I am "accepting something I shouldn't accept." I guess she resents my obsession with Irene.

JUNE 2
MUNICH

It's my first night alone here. Nanna's lover, Michael, is back, and she is with him. I am glad she is happy.

Since I am here, we've gone to the Nachteule club a couple of times. I love being surrounded by these tall Germans. We've walked in the Englischer Garten and eaten pancakes in the sun, read Mickey Spillane while a band played Viennese waltzes. Yesterday, I went for a riding lesson and watched myself in the stable mirror, sitting very straight, with flushed cheeks, my hair swinging. It was like a carousel, going round and round with the riding master, small, bald and red-faced, swearing and gesturing in the center. My back is a bit sore today, but only a little considering I haven't been on a horse in so long.

Nanna has kept all my letters from years ago. Those from Black Mountain are very interesting. Did I get that sheen, that worldliness, that assurance from Peggy, or was I really that sophisticated? The incident of my dropping a tray of dishes in the dining hall: "Everybody laughed, except Peggy." It sounds right but I don't really remember it. Nick Muzenic made me sit down while he picked up all the pieces.

I do remember Anni Albers saying, "She looks like art" about me. So flattering.

Every so often, I get a twinge in my stomach remembering the situation with Irene. But I have to resist it. After all, I survived Peggy!

LATER

I'm reading letters from 1950-51, from Paris, Ischia, Bel-Air. It is clear from them that I was not in love with Sven, but they exude a certain calm happiness that might be better than this turmoil. In 1952, I wrote, "The love of friends, and friends to love, is more important to me than love, lovers, etc." I had been thinking of Katherine Pfriem and Martin, but the truth is, I was really in love with both of them!

JUNE 10

I got back from Munich Monday, and my darling left for Italy today. When I got into town at midnight, Alberto told me she had already gone, and my face burned, and I could hardly get the phone to work. But she actually left this morning (Friday). On Monday night, she wept and said there are two of me, one she loves and one she hates.

SUNDAY JUNE 12

Last night I went to the Montagne [dyke bar] and made a date with a girl for next week, which I immediately regretted. I really dislike being the aggressor and giving some girl the chance to reject me. She is attractive and, in an abstract sort of way, I'd like to sleep with her, but I also sense that she is a cold bitch and would put me in the male role, which I dislike.

I spent the afternoon at Elliot Stein's [writer and film critic]. His fussiness is annoying. The story he showed me was gripping, but his fascination with sadism rather horrifies me. On my way home, I stopped in to see Pat Lane, who is going quite bald. She is one of the more repulsive people I have known. but I still get this perverse desire to see her once in a while (reminds me of San Francisco probably).

Ten p.m.

Had a solitary dinner, which I quite enjoyed. Then I met Dominique, who has broken up with his girl-friend. Too bad we are not at all attracted to each other. He might like to go to bed with me, but I am feeling calm and independent and would rather not.

June 14

It's a warm, hazy day. Nissan and Jacob are across the street from my hotel painting the façade of the bookstore. I can see that Jacob is enjoying working outside, feeling like a performer. He keeps looking up at my window, but luckily, his eyesight is not good.

No letter from Irene.

A man is singing mournfully for money; the neighbor's piano tinkles; a woman passes, carrying a bouquet of radishes in one hand and, in the other, a basket of strawberries.

This is my street, the *rue de Seine*.

FIVE P.M.

The barges go peacefully by, with their white, pink, and blue clotheslines waving. An old man with a white beard is sitting next to me on this bench. He masturbates furtively whenever he thinks I am looking. His face is expressionless, with one white eyeball. When another man comes to sit down, he moves away. He walks with difficulty, as though his balls were swollen. Is he trying to keep his erection?

Now back in my room, watching the young girl across the street who looks exactly like a Renoir. She is plump and pink-cheeked, with thick hair in bangs and a long, heavy braid in back. She is entertaining two dark, seedy-looking boys with glasses and mustaches, serving them from a tiny bottle of cognac. She sits next to the window, and her rosy cheeks and gold-brown hair glow in the evening sun. How romantic! How Parisian!

JUNE 16

Last night, out with Pat Lane, I got really drunk on three bottles of Munich beer. She was high too. I like her better that way. She said that Peter (the handsome Pole) thinks I am wonderful, beautiful, etc., and asked how he could get in touch with me. He seems to be involved in several simultaneous affairs.

I saw the great film star, Françoise Rosay, in the bar on the quay last night.

JUNE 17

Postcard from Irene—sweet but uncommunicative.

Went to the Montagne last night and was stood up. I danced with a very young, pretty girl who was also very scared. Met another girl, who told me that she "just likes to lie back and enjoy it." She is very happy with her "*amie*" because she, the friend, hates to be touched. That's the really dreary side of lesbian sex—girls who just want to be masturbated or sucked and give nothing back. With us, everything is mutual. . .

JUNE 19

Lonely. Bored. Unloved. Two years ago, I was loved and felt alive, thanks to Sven. Now, thanks to Irene, I am like this!

JUNE 21

Herta just left, and I am still shaking. She started to cry, and I changed the subject. It was stupid of me; I should have hurt her more. And telling me she had fallen in love with me the first time she met me—lying down on the bed and begging me to join her. I just wanted her to leave, the traitor! She has betrayed both of us, me and Irene!

JULY 1, 1955

At lunch, Evelyne called me an "eternal adolescent" and advised me to return to the States. Of course, I disagree.

Armand Drucker, the rich old man I met in St.-Tropez who called me a "*fausse maigre*" (a false thin person), called this morning to invite me on a trip to Brittany. He had awakened me, and I wasn't thinking and turned him down. I started regretting it, but now I feel I did the right thing. That's my new rule, "Never do things you don't really want to do."

Had an idea for a story about a sophisticated expatriate woman in New York, with her dying mother, who picks up a young man in a bar [Peter F.].She feels superior to him, his simplicity, his crudeness, but he gives her the first great orgasm of her life. She rejects him and returns to Europe, and then, in her loneliness, her memory transforms him. She realizes that, along with her mother's death, Peter has been the agent of her own sexual rebirth.

July 3

I had been planning to sleep with Dominique last night but from the start, everything worked against it. He wanted us to go to his apartment right away, before we went to the Bal Nègre but I said no. Dancing with the Negroes at the club, I was getting turned on, but there really is no chemistry between us. One problem with Dominique is that he talks too much, intellectualizes everything, keeps trying to be spontaneous, which, of course, doesn't work.

July 15
With Irene in Florence

Early morning in the youth hostel. Girls are stringing beads, braiding hair, sewing on buttons, putting bras on young white breasts. They speak every language.

Yesterday, we were in Sienna and stayed at the Tre Donzelle where I'd stayed with Sven. There were no silver birds in the cathedral. Did I dream that? Firenze is, as always, beautiful.

It is raining. Dear God, let things stay simple between us.

LATE JULY
PESARO, ITALY

Sitting in the sun on the hotel terrace. Peaches ripen on the concrete floor. The hills are green, fuzzy with grape vines and pointed with cypresses. The sea is very blue. Irene has gone down to the beach. I stay here because I have my period and because I really want to be alone. We are going through one of those dangerous episodes, when (my thoughts are running way ahead as I write this, and I question the truth of what I say before I even put it down) she is very dependent on me. Is that true or fair? Maybe she is just feeling close to me.

This morning, we made love in the dormitory—what a crazy thing to do!

JULY 25
PESARO

I have a terrible sunburn.
Tomorrow we move on. One odd thing—an attractive Swedish guy was coming on to me. I was confused by Irene's reaction. Men are going to keep on being a problem for both of us. I am afraid to sleep around, because I don't want her to. She probably feels the same way about me.

AUGUST 2, 1955
VERONA, ITALY

We are in a big blind square with the Church of St. Zeno. We stayed in the house of a South American woman named Anice, who might be the loneliest person I've ever met—childless, married out of her language, keeps cats. To me she seems half mad.

AUGUST 12,
BARCELONA, SPAIN

We are in the same pension, Segre, where Sven and I stayed three years ago. It's the same Rambla's, the same statue of Columbus that pointed me out to sea when I sailed away from him. Being here with Irene is strange. She sees things so differently than the way he did, more tenuously. We seem to melt into places rather than storming them as Sven and I did. Soon, we leave for Ibiza. I am a little fearful about it. Will it have been crushed by tourists? Will we find a house where we can be free, we two, little girls?

AUGUST 19
IBIZA, SPAIN

Sitting on the *mole* in the sun. Plop and glunk of water, kissing fish-like on the stone. All day, I hear

Sven's name, people asking about *el señor*, the Ibicencos and the scandal-seeking expatriates. It's much easier to be in a straight couple here. So far, they don't *get* Irene and me. She is acting strangely, lacking initiative, tired. I am often impatient with her. Once, when I was with Sven, I wrote, "I'd rather be with a woman if I have to run things. . ." How ironic! People speak admiringly of Sven, making me feel like a discarded wife.

Ibiza is still the most beautiful place I know—the rocks, the green and silver trees, that brilliant blue sea. Everything pleases me here, and I feel very much at home. I just wrote Sven. I know he will be hurt.

In Barcelona, I bought a charming new notebook, thick cardboard covers, mottled red and black, with a green binding. I feel a compulsion to finish this one. Perhaps, in the end, my life's work will be these school notebooks full of faded words. *Diary of a Nobody*, or *The Fall of an Angel*.

AUGUST 20
IBIZA

Winter threatens me and nothing done. Grasshopper knocking at the ant's door. "*Jeunesse passe, mademoiselle*" the man in the café repeated. I have achieved nothing. And one day, I will go underground with wormy things and roots. Icon: a diving girl. When the ink has faded on these pages, I will be old or dead.

August 24

Thunder and cock crow. Loud sea. Heavy Tintoretto clouds. In my Last Judgement, whom will I send to heaven, to hell? Peter, Irene, Sven, Peggy?

In the other room, Irene sits on the bed with her legs spread, writing a play.

Across the Calle de la Virgen, the old lady behind her fishnet curtain sings through her nose, "Un caballito. . ." The wind is frivolous.

Now, I will try again to write about my mother's funeral.

My sister and I went in to view our mother before anyone else saw her, especially my father, Mr. Faintheart. She was waiting for us, in a private room at the funeral parlor, with her name on the door. On entering, the odor of her corpse covered our faces like a shroud. It was a large, carpeted room with maple-stained furniture. A lamp stood on a table, illuminating an open leather-bound book, with empty pages for mourners to sign. There were many vases full of flowers, and chairs arranged in rows like in the waiting room of a dentist's office.

At the back of the room, was another piece of furniture a long, walnut coffin. Looking into it, at first, all we could see was a pile of white gauze, like a mound of snow. And deep within it lay a shrunken head, yellowish-white with an enormous beak, wrinkled, sunken, black-circled eyelids, and a tiny, puckered mouth. She had no chin. . .cancer and the

surgeons had seen to that. . .and a narrow little forehead, with purple dents at its sides, almost hidden in
gauze. That head was not hers; it was a wax model
or a Halloween mask! Or a rotten, faded, hard-boiled
egg. In no way did that thing resemble the head of
my mother. As for her powerful, big-breasted, heavy-
bellied body, it had been ironed out flat, like a wafer,
first by cancer and then by the finicky doll-makers in
the embalming department. My sister and I fell back
in horror, as they say, shrieking and covering our
eyes. We ran out of the room into the cool, imitation-
marble hallway, calling for whomever was in charge,
the one responsible: "Close the coffin!" we shouted,
"Close the coffin!" When we found the tall, sad-looking director of the funeral parlor, we told him we
wanted the coffin closed. No one else in this world
should ever have to witness that hideous thing. . .

I am making myself miserable thinking of departures, goodbyes: a vision of farewells on this gray,
thundery afternoon, while the sea slaps against the
walls of the town. And now, suddenly, I feel: why go
back to Paris? Why not stay right here?

WEDNESDAY AUGUST 27

I dreamed of a visit to Garbo. A line of people, mostly
women, were waiting to see her. I am very dowdy, in
my worn sheepskin coat. But when I am admitted
to her audience room, I suddenly become beautiful,

with long, dark hair swept over one shoulder. She is ugly—sharp cheekbones, blotchy skin, small black eyes. She wants me to work for her as her maid. I keep studying her face, expecting it to become beautiful.

Second dream: I am in a youth hostel. In the cot next to me is Groucho Marx. He flirts with me in a fatherly way. I find him very attractive. Irene tells me his daughter is a lesbian.

THURSDAY, AT THE *ESTRELLITA*

It's very crowded here today; people sitting all around me talking loudly. I am thinking about Juliette Greco, whom Parisians say I resemble. One day, she will be remembered best for her role in Cocteau's movie *Orphée*, before she had her nose job.

Irene and I were renting an apartment on the ground floor of a house in the Calle de la Virgen, across from the brothel. Two nights ago, we forgot to cover the barred windows onto the street, and a group of teenaged boys watched us making love. They began yelling, and throwing dirt and pebbles into the room, and calling us whores. Last night, they came back, and I chased them down the street while the prostitutes watched from their balcony. My stomach was so tight with anger and fear, it actually hurt. It felt good, though, to fight back, to frighten them and call them cowards. Today we are in a new apartment, with brown-and-yellow tiled floors and a balcony. We are sleeping in separate rooms. We saved two kittens abandoned in the street. We are calling them Fred Astaire and Ginger Rogers.

Monday Morning

I am having coffee at the *Estrellita*, sitting in the spot where the little German lesbian, Brigitta, threw up last night all over herself while her pretty friend, Dorothy, called her a pig.

Saturday

Yesterday, Irene's trunk arrived from the south, with all her beautiful dresses and souvenirs and love letters, many of them from me. They are painfully disturbing to both of us. I'd like to destroy all of mine, right now, while she is sleeping.

Yesterday, she said, "How much I was in love with you! What a shame you turned out to be such a bitch!"

I'm nervous about going back to Paris. I think she will want to stay here, and that is probably a good idea.

Fiesta at Jesus this morning. When I came out

of the mass, Byron said to me, "The first time I saw you in Ibiza, I thought of the song, "Si tu t'imagines" . . .It's about *jeunesse passe,* Mlle. as the man at the Monaco was always telling me. Byron said there is something so careless about me, so unhurried, but, he warns me, time does rush.

Loose thoughts:

A fish eye is nature's marble. When cooked, it is white, nature's Ping-Pong ball.

"*Gatito muerto para vender. Quien quiere comprar un gatito muerto?*"

The broken one-note lullaby of the old woman next door seems to come from before the invention of music.

My sister has had two abortions. Irene too. I've never had any.

Shouts from the street. Irene is reading a funny magazine. She chuckles. Contentment in the eyes of the black cat.

Long sleeps, orgasms, swimming between the waves, hot baths, bacon and eggs, books.

At the restaurant, they offered us bull's testicles for lunch., skinned, pink, shaped like canteens. Held in the hand and pinched gently. . .

I am feeling very alone with Irene, at her mercy.

Last night at Alan's (ugh) party, I sang and sang.

SITTING ON THE SEAFRONT

The Barcelona boat is coming with some of the returning expats, like Ernst Ehrenfeld (the person who first told Sven and me about Ibiza at the Dôme in Montparnasse) and the tough German woman called Isabel. It is a cool, wet morning; summer is nearly over. I am thinking of spending the winter here with Irene. It's easier living than in Paris. But the two German girls, Dorothy and Brigitta, are trouble. I am getting too old for these games.

LATER, AT THE *KIOSKO*

The café is full of people waiting for the boat. The port police stand around with folded arms and sunglasses, chatting. A little boy retrieves the silver foil from a pack of Lucky Strikes from under my chair. We slept all afternoon.

SEPTEMBER 17

Rainy weather. I begin to see it would be impossible to spend the winter here with Irene and all these crazy small town scandals.

SEPTEMBER 19

I am leaving soon. When I'm gone, Irene will sleep with the pretty young Canadian boy. The fucking German girls stay on and on.

END OF SEPTEMBER

End of us. She is still sleeping, smiling, dreaming, perhaps about Dorothy. How absurd it all is—these terrible parties and this terrible end of summer.

LATER

I am in Santa Eulalia, where I have come to get away from things until Dorothy leaves, supposedly on Saturday. (Oh God, make her go!) I am sitting on a hill-top, looking down on the so-blue sea, the red earth, the golden trees. At this moment, Irene is most likely in bed, making love to Dorothy.

Some of this is my fault, of course. When I took Brigitta to bed, it was partly a joke, partly revenge. I didn't really want to. I forced myself. The poor thing was all excited but she couldn't come. She was probably feeling my impatience and cruelty. I loathe her!

FRIDAY
SANTA EULALIA

This is good. This is the best thing I've done in a long time. Sitting quietly in this fine house, with its landward and seaward windows, the dog and the cat.

I have had a great shock. After two years of total dependency and giving all my energy to this love—like trying to keep a match burning in a high wind—it is gone. We should have had a brief affair, but I have refused to see clearly and clung to it too long. I am addicted to her, but I must give it up, starting NOW. . .

LATER

After a heavy sleep, a heavy rain, I sit in the warm late-afternoon sun above the calm, pink sea like an invalid, reading *The New Yorker*.

BACK IN CIUDAD DE IBIZA

Almost to the end of this painful notebook; already estranged from Ibiza, from this house, the kittens, everything.

Irene is making chess pieces from little plaster squares molded in matchboxes. She plants shells, matches, beads in the tiny cubes. I am sick with the fear of being alone.

Two more days on this beloved island.

I tell myself, "Just keep walking with your eyes open."

Romaine Lorquet, sculptor

Sven Blomberg, painter

With Maria Irene Fornes
in Venice, Italy

Maria Irene Fornes,
playwright

With Susan Sontag in Germany

Susan Sontag in Athens, Greece

In Cadiz,
Spain

CADIZ

With Susan
and my sister
on the Bd. St.
Michel, Paris

With Ricardo Vigon
at the Cafe Flore,
Paris

Vezio in Elba,
Italy

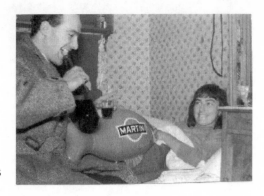

With Bruno in Paris

Back from abroad in
Provincetown, MA

Notebook Four

October 3, 1955
Paris

New notebook, new page, new room. I am in the Hôtel de Dieppe on the rue de l'ancienne-Comedie, a very busy street. It is a big room, with two big windows and a big bed, a good room for love. The whole hotel smells like sex. Maybe that's because I spent a night here with that Irishman a while ago.

This morning, Paris is gray with fog. The first familiar face I ran into on the Boulevard St.-Germain was someone from Ibiza. What a drag!

October 4, morning

Now to begin a new life of resourcefulness.

Rule I: Do not wait for mail.

Rule II: Do not waste time imagining her life.

Action is good. Last week in Ibiza, I was dying of a slow poison. But first the boat, then Barcelona, then the train and finally—finding the room, finding my friends, the daylight of Paris—all have helped me. Am I a bit afraid? Sure.

Last night, I saw Elliott [Stein] and Richard [Olney] at the Reine Blanche. They loved my brown-velour Ibiza suit. I love it too; it's like a friendly animal from the island.

Being alone is hard. I remember my mother saying, "Go out and play with the children," but there weren't any, or they didn't want to play with me. And then, when my sister came, she'd say, "Aren't you lucky; you have each other? You can never be lonely again." How wrong you were, Mom.

THURSDAY

Heavy rain glistens on the old slate roofs. I love my long view down rue Dauphine across the pont Neuf, to the imposing prow of the Samaritaine department store with its golden sign.

I have been noticing the masculine quality of Parisian girls. Not only are there many young, studious-looking lesbians, but numerous others who seem straight but stride along in leather jackets and short hair, strong and boyish. It is especially striking in contrast with the super-femininity of the Spanish girls.

Got my first letter from Irene, lonely and nostalgic. She's probably over it by now. In a window across the street, there is a cage full of yellow canaries, jumping about and swinging on their perches.

They look like sunbeams.

I saw Han yesterday. He is beautiful and intelligent, but there is something self-hating going on in him. His wife is rather dreary; with those big eyes and big tits, she still looks starved.

Passing the Mabillon this morning, I caught a glimpse of Raymond [Mason] looking pale, thin, and old. And so, some eat, and some are eaten.

LATER

Still room; still, broad bed; key hanging strangely still from the keyhole; the ring, with its British coin dangling, casts a lovely shadow.

FRIDAY

The French are a nasty-minded people who don't believe in innocence and interpret everything in a nasty way.

Sam liked my Ibiza piece.

SATURDAY

Went to the *Cinémathèque* last night, where there is a wonderful exhibition of old movie memorabilia. Some things I especially liked were: the embroidered self-portrait of Asta Nielsen, the cardboard vampire lying on a red velvet couch, the big blow-up of Garbo in *Anna Christie*, Barrault's Pierrot costume from *Les Enfants du Paradis*, and the many pictures of actors I didn't recognize—with their enormous eyes, shadowy cheekbones, and eccentric, claw-like hands, the women with big, wild heads of curly hair. Very beautiful.

They were showing Stroheim's *Greed*. It oozes erotic imagery, linking the woman's avarice to her sexual fears. How wonderful the wedding party, with the little hunchback nibbling a creamy cake, flakes of it all over his mouth, the priest's thin bone, the fat, brutal couple gobbling animal heads, teeth and all!

SUNDAY

Last night, I went out with Martha Strater and her lover, Pat. Martha is still the same shallow, scared, hypocritical person. Pat is a complete monster, a snob, a hater, a bitch. She said, "Let's be friends, Harriet. I like you," and a little later, after a few drinks, "I don't like you, Harriet. You're nothing." She still resents that I never came on to her, that Martha is always praising me, that Irene finally rejected her that night in New York. She has that WASP money complex. "You went to the wrong schools, girl!" Those people either love me or hate me. Thank God Richard [Olney] was with me to help me laugh at her.

MONDAY

I ran into Paul Szasz in Orestias restaurant. He talks
of nothing but himself, his illness, his symptoms. I
detected a certain weird joy in him; maybe just having an audience makes him happy. He says he for-
gets his troubles when he eats. He shakes when he
speaks, and his face looks dirty; crumbs in the corners of his mouth, blotchy nose and cheeks. It made
me slightly nauseous, and I became impatient with
him and left.

There is a picture of Peggy in her bar, The Tin
Angel, in Holiday magazine. A letter from Irene.

WEDNESDAY, AT AMERICAN EXPRESS

Nothing from Irene; a sweet note from Nanna. "I
hope you and Irene will not pick up again right away.
Darling, I am sure you need not be unhappy without
her, without a woman. Don't screw a lot of monsters
right away. . . (I mean alcoholics, premature ejacula-
tors, etc.)."

THURSDAY

Last night, I dreamed I was back in Ibiza, and she
didn't want me there. I felt ashamed. But every day
frees me from her a little bit more. I imagine her sur-

rounded by the expat crowd, who all wanted her. And Dorothy, the German bitch!

I ran into Iliazd, the old painter who is in love with Irene. He hates me. I think he feels I stand between them, although he must be aware of how unattractive he is. He makes me uneasy, and I find myself trying to prove something to him. How stupid!

FRIDAY, OCTOBER 13, 1955

No letter. I wake up later each day, avoiding the life. Last night I was at the Select, which has become much more beautiful now that the other cafés have gotten so modern/ugly.

There are the big potted plants and an old style that is very agreeable. Only: whenever I am there, I feel a certain fear that something or someone from the past will jump out at me. So many memories and connections are hanging there in the smoke—Sven, Herta, Irene. . . I ran into Marie-Pierre [Humbert] who asked if I see Herta. There's something sinister in her, despite her beauty. Also met Marisol [sculptor], a beautiful Venezuelan girl from New York. She has a strange quietness that is disconcerting.

Had a letter from Sven saying that, of course I can go with them to the Mediterranean. I suspect it would be terribly awkward.

2:00 A.M.

Dreamed of Rosita's brothel in Ibiza. I wanted to sleep with a girl, but the madam wouldn't let me. Much embarrassment.

Yesterday, I went to see someone with a room to rent in her apartment in the Madeleine neighborhood. She was a big, fat, vulgar (Jewish?), middle-class woman. Her place was full of Chinese bric-a-brac. She seemed sensual, indiscreet and lonely. She said, "*Vous êtes une très belle fille. Pourquoi ne cherchez-vous a se marier?*" I lied and said I had been married (which I was, in a way). I couldn't possibly live there, although the bathtub and hot water certainly attracted me.

Was out tonight, wandering aimlessly. Had a long, gossipy chat with the *patronne* at the Hôtel Verneuil (Elliott's hotel) and a delicious meal at la Chaumière. Ended up at the Bonaparte talking to an American Negro who wanted to fuck, but he was so graceless and lacking in charm, that I came home and worked on the translation. Now, I hope I can get some sleep.

MONDAY OCTOBER 16

Dreamed last night of blowing John Ashbery! It woke me up. I think what has put me in this state is the last letter from Irene, in which she speaks so tenderly of my suffering that final week in Ibiza. Hadn't she realized the depth of my love for her?

Then the letter from that damn Brigitta, so pathetic and stupid, brought back the whole miserable business. She pleads with me to write her, "Don't be so hard and wright (sic) to me. . ." I tore up the letter and flushed it down the toilet. So much for the problem of whether to answer it.

The dream about Ashbery last night was clearly a result of my need for sex. Going down on a faggot is not my idea of fun.

TUESDAY OCTOBER 18

The cold weather has really set in, that luminous, bone-chilling grayness, which I have only known in London and Paris. It's so cold in my room that I am wearing my beloved striped scarf (Sven's gift) and gloves. It's bad to be alone in this kind of weather. Last night, Lydia said she must get herself *"un amour bouillotte,"* a hot-water-bottle love. Me too. The streets are quite deserted, even the busy rue de Buci, and the Samaritaine seems to be wearing a gray veil.

THURSDAY

Last night I saw *Le chien andalou* and *L'Age d'or,* early surrealist films by Buñuel and Dali. I especially loved the first, where the man slices the woman's eyeball as a cloud bisects the moon.

I am not in my right mind these days. Yesterday, I wandered all over rue St.-Honoré and the *place Vendôme*, fantasizing that someone like Coco Chanel would see me and hire me as a model.

EVENING

This afternoon, Joann Chatelin (an American expat married to a Frenchman) came over, and we took a long walk in the sunshine. I find her attractive, although a bit dull. She said people never remember her, though she always remembers them.

Had another letter from Irene today telling me she slept with Erwin Broner because she felt sorry for him. "People are so pitiful and alone." I really resent her Earth Mother number, her overflowing compassion for people; it's so fake. But I can't tell her that, for fear she'll get angry and stop writing. The only letter I really want is the one that says, "Come back to me."

OCTOBER 1, FRIDAY NIGHT

Sven and Romaine here today. About the idea of a threesome, two men and a woman, she remarked "*Quelle bonne idée.*" When I said to Sven, "*Tu n'as pas de maladies imaginaires parce que tu n'as pas d'imagination!*" she exclaimed, "*Ca c'est belle!*" Her strong handshake, her flirtatiousness. Is she dangerous to Sven? To me?

SATURDAY NIGHT, OCTOBER 30

A month since I left Ibiza; the moon is full again, shining right into my little window. It must be wonderful on the island where she is warm and loved. I am feeling lonely and sorry for myself. Funny how much taller I feel when I am lonely. I remember the stupid criticism of that snotty NYU boy when I submitted my story, "Tight Ceilings," to the literary magazine: "Couldn't you give some other reason for her loneliness than her height?" As though another were needed . . .

HALLOWEEN

Peggy's son was born today in 1948. That makes him seven. That glorious night I went Halloweening in Berkeley with a gang of fags, all of us in costume. We were stopped on the Bay Bridge by a cop. . .James Broughton [avant-garde film maker] and his lover Kermit Sheets. They are still together now in Paris. Seven years! And I was groped by a guy at the party who thought I was male. What a shock for him!

Last night, when I couldn't get to sleep, I tried thinking of something pleasant. They say that helps, but I kept coming up with awful things. . .my mother's illness, her death, Irene in bed with someone else.

I tried to focus on last year; Harry, and how he phoned me every day at lunchtime just to hear my voice. How he kissed my feet in the shower and said, "I've never given myself so completely to any woman," and the postcard he sent filled entirely with the words "I love you."

Yes, yes, being loved; how beautiful it makes you. Sometimes suffering does that too. The night I left Ibiza she said, "You are radiant. I look around at other people, and then at you, and you are much more beautiful." And the day before, the last time we made love (forever?), she said, "No one knows your real beauty who hasn't made love to you. . ."

And then, Peter in New York, who was not in love but admired me as a sophisticated, older woman and gave me the best time in bed I'd ever had. Now he's married.

I was in love with Harry for a minute, after the first time we made love, and he went home to his wife, and I lay in bed, drowning in emotion, listening to music—Shostakovich, Saint-Saëns, that once, only.

NOVEMBER 1

"Memoirs of a Failure," "Memoirs of a Hard-living Lady," "Homesickness," "The Homeless."

Sven came tonight. There's comfort in being with him, even when he bores me. Tired of hanging around with homos. Elliott is getting on my nerves. Got the curse.

NOVEMBER 3

Ricardo (Vigón) said my smile is like an *éventail*, a fan. Last night, trying to remember what he said, I almost said *épouvantail*, scarecrow.

MONDAY

With some young Americans at the Café Tournon— scared, dumb boys, scared of sex, of thinking, of reality. One hid behind, "All I want to do is make a buck." Another, "Here we are talking about the world and we haven't got twenty francs in our pockets," which wasn't even true, of course. How upset they were when the French boy, the only intelligent one in the group, started talking about erections. One, mumbling, "I didn't hear what you said," and then, "I never had an erection. The Korean girls didn't appeal to me. . ." Poor boy, pimples, buck teeth—poor, fucked-up Americans!

TUESDAY

A letter from Irene—sweet, kind, telling me I must come to Ibiza if I want, and that "if we find we cannot live in the same place," she will leave.

WEDNESDAY
AMSTERDAM

It's a dark, cold city, with canals, barges, running children, seagulls. I am lying on a bed *chez* Bertus; the long-nosed, noble-jawed mathematician sits at his table, working. I had such hopes of him last night, but now he seems to have shied away from me and has not repeated his invitation for me to stay here tonight. I guess I'll have to go out in the cold to a café and pick somebody up.

Bertus is a forlorn old bachelor, with soft, thinning hair and a noble head, who will turn strange in ten years, lonely, like Paul Szasz.

Ran into Gershon Legman this morning at the museum. What a phony! He showed me a Hindu statue of a woman and said it was the first time he'd seen a clitoris on a piece of sculpture. Gave me a long explanation about matriarchal societies; how men perform cunnilingus for hours (his thing, I've always suspected), and the woman's orgasm is the most important.

Poor Legman, so unattractive and knowing too much about things to be interesting. His wife must despise him. Women have contempt for men who understand them too well and worship them too much. Matriarchy? How would that be? Certainly much sexier and more peaceful than it is now.

I'm reading magazines while Bertus works. Found a really bad story by Elizabeth Pollet—overly-stylish, falsely philosophical and objective, while really totally personal. Beautiful, blonde Elizabeth, in her brown fur coat in Washington Square, married to Delmore Schwartz.

Bertus suddenly resuming an earlier conversation, asks, "Are men and women enemies?" I reply, "More often than they should be." Then, just as suddenly, he goes back to work.

My Last Night in Amsterdam

It has been lovely here, especially that first night with Bertus, his ardent and enthusiastic response. And the admiring friendliness of Witte and Susann, Eva and the others. That first night, walking home with him, a big man, that wonderful Dutch tallness!

Surely I belong in a northern place, with these slow, kind, tall, serious people.

NOVEMBER 22
PARIS

This damn cold chokes me. I feel tired and vague. The woman in Orestias restaurant today, with her thin, bony face, long nose, and wrinkles—dressed in a beautiful turquoise sweater and a plaid shawl—talking to herself. Tight, starved little mouth; maybe thirty-five—a tragic old maid. Dear God, preserve me from such a fate!

NOVEMBER 23

Saw Hanna [Ben-Dov, Israeli painter] and Reggie [Pollock, her husband, American painter] at the Reichel exhibition. Also, oddly, Diorka and Ivan Kats, together.

THURSDAY MORNING

Extraordinary dreams last night. They cling to my thoughts. In one, I am with Peggy, traveling some-where. Brigitta shows up. . .most embarrassing. She looks different, small and red-faced. Maybe it was really Irene.

Then I am in bed with a man and a woman. She is in the middle and starts making love to both of us, but the man won't play. She acts surprised. "Don't you do this?" she asks, and gestures with her hands to make a daisy chain. I laugh, but the man is annoyed. She leaves, and we go out to dinner. He says he only likes it *à deux*.

Then it is raining. My feet are wet. I buy a lottery ticket—any number ending in one. I spend two hundred francs, two very shiny hundred-franc coins. Money is pouring out from somewhere. I had a dream like this one night in Ibiza. . .Maybe money means orgasm?

I have a date with Nissan [Rilov, Israeli painter] tomorrow night.

FRIDAY NIGHT

Ugh! Nissan! One second of excitement paid for by three hours of boredom. Finally, I couldn't take it any more, and just left him suddenly at the Select. That wasn't very nice of me after he had bought me dinner and sped me around in taxis, but really, he is too ridiculous—like most men who squeeze your breasts until they hurt, rub your face raw with their unshaven cheeks, push it into you, and come, *et voilà!*

He tells me he was in love with me last year at the start of our boring affair. . . .What a drag!

SUNDAY

I slept with Polish Peter last night. The best moment (after the marvelous steaks), was opening my eyes after my first orgasm and finding him looking down at me, his face younger and very Slavic and pure satyr! I could swear even his ears were pointed. Otherwise, it wasn't much good. Had to go down on him for ages without a great result. However, he is beautiful, maybe the most beautiful man I've ever slept with.

WEDNESDAY

A growing, pathetic preoccupation with Polish Peter, who hasn't called. I keep wanting to phone him, but I know that would be a mistake. I keep going over the events of that night, and, especially my stupid insistence on leaving him to keep my date with Nissan.

(Damn fool! How I hate him, though he is kind and good.)

Interviewing for the job at the *International Herald Tribune.*

SATURDAY DECEMBER 4

No word from Peter. I phoned today, my heart galloping, but he was out. Left a message, but he hasn't called. Clear enough. Had a letter from Irene saying, "I'm thinking of coming to Paris for Christmas. Will you be there?"

I rather hope she doesn't come. The only good thing about my misery and loneliness is that she is not around to witness it.

Tonight I am going with Pat Lane and her new girlfriend to a dyke bar. I'd do almost anything not to spend the night alone, so I'll have to go. She's leaving Europe soon, thank God. My relationship with her has always been ugly, but sometimes I get desperate for company.

DECEMBER 6

Settling into my job at the *Trib.*
Posed for Hanna again today. She is very interested in lesbians; tells me her best friend was one. She likes me, and I am attracted to her, but that will never happen. Too many connections.

Spent the weekend with Pat, her beautiful Dutch girl, Miep (who flirted with me and got me hot), and a little American girl, sweet, hungry, and unattractive. We drove to Chartres.

DECEMBER 9

I'm so tired of loving Irene and of that awful anxiety I feel when I hear of someone going to Ibiza and meeting her. Of course, it's inevitable that she will fall in love again, probably before I do. I doubt she will come here at Christmas and what would be the point of it? We would make love and feel sad and say goodbye again.

DECEMBER 11

Last night, the little American girl, Valerie, slept here. She is sweet, but so scared and screwed up. Has never had an orgasm. When I got her almost there, she panicked and closed her legs, fought against it, so it didn't happen. I peed in my chamber pot in front of her, and she looked away and refused to use it herself. Pathetic. . .

Now Miep, the Dutch girl, that's a whole other matter. We both got hot just dancing together.

DECEMBER 12

It's the anniversary of my mother's death. A cold, dark day. I have the *cafard* (blues) and a pain in my breast.

Downstairs, there were two letters from Irene sounding unhappy and reproachful. Too bad!

I went to the Courtauld exhibition and saw some paintings so beautiful they almost made me cry. Some small Seurats, a ravishing Cézanne, a Manet of men working in a snowy street. . .so Parisian! Also, a wonderful Modigiliani nude, with long, stringy hair and closed eyes. She looks like me.

Then, on my way to Amex, I was stopped by a big handsome American who said he knew me from Black Mountain College. His name is Galway Kinnell, and I've read some of his poetry. We had coffee together, and I'm sure I made a poor impression on him, feeling so desperate and not in my *assiette,* as the French say.

At Amex, I had a Chanukah card from Dad with a ten dollar bill in it. Also, a story I sent to *Botteghe Oscure*, wildly confident they would take it, came back. And a sad, sick letter from Harry, bitter and gray, like the weather.

Had a lousy lunch at Orestias and coffee at the Old Navy. Back at the hotel, they told me a tall man had come to see me. It was probably Sven, but could it have been Peter?

Then, off to work.

I have a job at the *International Herald Trib*, transcribing stories called in by the correspondents in Moscow, London, Bonn, etc. My hours are great . . . six p.m. to midnight, perfect for a night person like me. The office is on rue de Berri, right off the

Champs-Élysées, sort of a glamorous neighborhood. It has given a welcome structure to my crazy life, as well as a regular paycheck.

TUESDAY

I posed for Hanna again today, and it was lovely. Do I just like posing so much, or is it her powerful presence that I enjoy? I left her atelier—and the Pernod and the vision of her smoking that slim clay pipe in a state of exaltation—feeling beautiful. At the *Trib* office, I wrote a sketch for the New York/mother novel I'm planning.

WEDNESDAY

It is a dark, rainy day, and I woke up at noon. I am trying to write while certain images obsess me— empty Miami avenues, heat rising from the baking blacktop as I wait for the bus beside a tall lamppost, wearing makeup and a summer dress. The unreality of it.

SUNDAY DECEMBER 18

Dancing with Pat's girl, Miep, last night at the Montagne. She whispered, "I love you; I love you more

than her," in my ear. "Will you write to me?" I answered, "All I want to do is sleep with you!" And she
replied, "No, that's not true. . ."

She wanted me to come to her today, but in
spite of my dislike of Pat, I couldn't do that, betray
her! If Miep wants me, she will have to come here.

DECEMBER 20

It's the coldest day of this cold winter. Yet Irene is
leaving the warmth of Ibiza to come here.

Hanna called this morning to cancel my mod-
eling session and I'm very disappointed. Her voice
on the phone was cool and the Israeli accent much
stronger than when I am with her. So I lie on the narrow bed in my garret thinking about how to see Miep
again before she leaves for Holland.

I bought Nanna a birthday present and sent it off
to Munich. It's a delicate necklace of tiny irregular
coral beads, very sweet (500 francs). I'd love to have
one just like it.

DECEMBER 21

Irene is here and more beautiful than ever. She fills
my life with heat and movement, perilous orgasms.
Everything torments me—the house where she is

staying, the hours she spends with others. . .I must keep my head!

JANUARY 3, 1956

Resolved: Not to encourage Irene's relationships by focusing on them, seeing them as more important than they are. . .

JANUARY 21

She is gone again. I drift back to earth.

The other night, I went to bed with Alberto [Greco] and a beautiful blond boy with a face like an *enfant terrible* and a long smooth body. His birthday is March 24th, two days before mine, and he comes from St. Quentin, where Richard [Olney] and I spent the night en route to Holland. The best moment of the *partouze* was when they were each sucking on a breast. . .delicious sensation.

Had a letter from Miep. Perhaps I will visit her.

Yesterday, Sven and Romaine were here, and he fell asleep on my bed while R and I talked. She was looking very dykey with her tweed suit, heavy shoes, cropped hair. She is beautiful. I'd like to sleep with her and although I see that she loves Sven she is perhaps, nevertheless, attracted to me.

JANUARY 28

Last week I had another surprising sexual encounter. It was with Claude, a tall, heavy, gray-haired guy. I was totally bombed, but I seem to remember he was very good, big and knowing. There was a kind of sweetness and reserve about him that I liked. He said, "*Tu baises bien!*" (You fuck well).

I didn't see him again until last night at the Bonaparte, where he totally ignored me. Of course, I started to feel that faint love which always accompanies rejection of my still adolescent self. He left with a group of people for the *États-Unis* in Montparnasse. I was alone and slightly high and feeling that reckless energy I've been experiencing lately that's gotten me into bed with perfect strangers in the last ten days.

I went to the *Reine Blanche* and there was that Algerian boy who calls himself Ricardo.

He is very handsome, tall and brown. I took him with me to the *États-Unis* where the crowd all was: Claude, Nina Engel, Sima, etc. Everyone except Claude greeted me warmly. He just looked away. There was good jazz and a fine atmosphere, and the beautiful Arab boy was kissing and caressing me. Eventually, around six a.m. I brought him home, and we made love for hours. He is not very talented but, thankfully, very hot. This afternoon he said, "*Tu fais très bien l'amour, tu sais?*" I said I did know.

I sure hope none of this has knocked me up.

That ignorant Arab had insanely removed my diaphragm without saying a word. Luckily, I checked and douched a lot. I wonder what he thought it was? When I finally got rid of him, I went to the *bains-douches* and took a hot bath. I lay a long time in the grayish water; came home smelling of perfumed soap and went luxuriously to bed.

Had coffee at the Old Navy, where a pretty but morbidly pale girl was giving me the eye.

As Irene once pointed out, being flirted with by a woman in a straight setting is very flattering. Now I'm going to Joann's party, which will most likely be a bore. Had a note from Otto Ranschburg with 3,000 francs in it, saying, "Sorry pal; this is all that was left."

This was the elderly Viennese rare book dealer I worked for in New York. He had a sort of crush on me and contacted me when he came here on business. He took me out to dinner, clubs, etc.; a charming man but very short and very old. (I think he hoped I would sleep with him.)

JANUARY 30

Well, I'm bleeding up a storm, so my rash promiscuity was not punished. Joann's party was a drag, as I expected, very uptight bourgeois.

This afternoon, I'll begin translating Mr. Abkhazi's economics column at the *Trib*. He is a courtly old Georgian gentleman who picked me for the job. I am flattered and determined to do it well.

FEBRUARY 1

Cold wave! Frost on the windows. No running water. They probably turned it off to keep the pipes from freezing. My hands are sticky from eating oranges, and my teeth want desperately to be brushed.

Sven came by this morning wearing his gray fur motorcycle gloves. He nags me to write. Irene too.

Thinking about one-night stands—how strange they are. To be so physically close to someone for a moment and then, in public places, to meet like strangers.

My co-worker at the *Trib*, Louisa, a very blonde Protestant, American type, has had two abortions. That surprises me, given her virginal look. She tells me about her lover, and I tell her about mine, disguising the gender, of course.

Tomorrow, I am going to visit Ricardo at the American Hospital.

FEBRUARY 5

How terrible it would be if Romaine and I fell in love! We both flirted like mad last night, and her knee pressing against my thigh under the table reminded me of that night three years ago in the movies, when I felt her leg against mine. And why does she ask me if I am a lesbian? Surely Sven has told her about my history. And what was that long, mysterious speech about not letting people get the goods on you. I could easily fall in love with her, but how evil that would be to dear Sven.

FEBRUARY 9

Last night, the threesome we've all been waiting for finally happened. It was obvious that they had made a plan, but it didn't work out as it should have. He constantly interfered, thrusting himself between us whenever we got really close. There was a certain pleasure in the soft, secret embraces we managed, but what was the point? She never let me take her to orgasm, and I felt like a toy they were playing with but not much interested in. I guess that was *it*! She's had me and his honor is saved. I guess I should feel guilty at having wanted to take her away from my dear old ex-lover but how I hated him when he grabbed my hands and pulled my mouth away from her breasts. And when he screwed me, I didn't feel a thing. Now, I know why I never enjoyed it with him; just too small! I always blamed it on myself. Oh well, she loves him. . .*tant mieux!*

FEBRUARY 17
JUST BACK FROM AMSTERDAM

In the trolley car, with heavy feathers of snow falling all around, Bertus said, "It's like a dream."

And in Rotterdam, there was Miep, with her artificial mannerisms, her hardness, her lies! She betrayed all Pat's pathetic secrets, and said, "I am afraid to sleep with you because I would fall in love with you!" Such a phony with her hidden claws!

Now, back in Paris in this mess with Sven and Romaine. She is being very friendly, asking about my adventures. I know she is playing some game with me, but I'm not sure what it is.

All I want is to have her here alone with me for a long afternoon. I'm sure she knows that, but then, what?

FEBRUARY 18

R called me at work last night. I told her what I want, and she said, yes, maybe tomorrow. Strangely, I am not concerned with Sven at all right now. I trust her, that she will handle it.

Algerian Ricardo is still around, bothering me. When I told him I am through with him, he hit me in rue de Buci, pushed me against a storefront and slapped me. I screamed for help, but nobody paid any attention. To the French, any woman with a connection to an Arab must be a whore and not worth their pity. I ran down rue de Seine to the hotel, but he pushed in after me, crushing me against the door. Luckily, the *patron* heard me yelling and chased him away, shouting racist insults. Note: This incident cost me my job when the French refused to renew my work permit. Obviously, connection to an Algerian is suspicious.]

SUNDAY, IN MY ROOM, WAITING FOR R

I'm reading Genet's *notre dame des fleurs*. It puts me into a mood of unreal passion. The other night, I saw the Pabst film *Loulou*. Miep looks a lot like Louise Brooks and seems to share her belief that she can flirt her way out of any situation. Of course, her seductiveness doesn't protect her from Jack the Ripper!

Romaine just called to say that she isn't coming and wants me to meet her at a café in Auteuil. That's definitely not what I wanted, having imagined a long, luxurious afternoon, embracing, lying on the bed, drinking gin; not necessarily making love. I guess I will go; can't refuse her anything.

Yesterday, I ran into Annette [Michelson] and Bernard [Frechtman]—Annette with her green hat, her rigid elegance, her fake British accent, and her beard, more and more noticeable and disturbing. Ricardo [Vigón] spotted it at once. She seems unnerved by my presence, for some unknown reason. Bernard is friendly, aging, ill-shaven, very masculine, very depressed. [He was Jean Genet's English translator. Committed suicide soon after this encounter].

NIGHT

Romaine kissed me on the lips in the metro. I said, "*Tu es folle!*" She said, "*Je m'en fous,*" and kissed me again. In the café, we drank grogs. She said, "*Je veux être tout le temps avec toi. Comment c'est possible?*"

FEBRUARY 21

Another day wasted waiting to hear from Romaine.

No letter from Irene.

At times like this, I am grateful for the *Herald Trib* job. At least it gets me out of my room. The girl I work with, a sweet WASPy blonde, is in an abusive relationship with a guy. She listens to my complaints about my lover with obvious compassion. Misery does love company. Of course, I refer to *him*, *he* and so on. I think she'd be upset if she knew it was a woman I am suffering over.

It's very cold, that damp, bone-chilling Paris cold. New York is never this bad. Sven and Romaine leave next week.

SUNDAY

No, they are not leaving yet; maybe not at all. When we are together, she stares at me so intensely, I am embarrassed. Well? *Tout ça ne rime à rien!* (Without rhyme or reason).

Later, I went to the Bonaparte and the whole cast was there—Claude, Ricardo V., Bandeira, Pablo, Pamela. . .juke box playing; drinking until six in the morning.

MONDAY

Last night we slept together, embracing, sweating, having bad dreams and bad sex. Neither one of us came. It was evil and stupid. She loves Sven; her passion for me is sick and false. It's no good; remember that!

TUESDAY

Too awful and ridiculous. . .I've got crabs! I must have caught them from Arab Ricardo who is always around staring at me with big sad eyes. I have probably given them to Romaine, so the jig is up! I do have to tell her, and then Sven will find out and punish us both.

And now this crazy business with Sam Menashe suddenly making verbal love to me. He is just too poetic; I don't trust him a bit and suspect he's queer anyway.

How absurd to be walking around with blue salve on my pussy, being told how beautiful I am.

MARCH 1, 1956

The first spring day! The trees are still bare in the parc du Vert-Galant but the sun is warm, and the birds are back.

I don't know how much longer I can stand this job! I guess I'll stick it out for two more months, and then, with the money I'll have saved, take off somewhere. With whom? Why Romaine, of course, just the two of us.

MARCH 4

Sick in bed with *la grippe*. Many people came to visit me yesterday; it was lovely and vanquished my usual fear of being ill and alone. Joann came first, bringing bread and butter and fruit. Then Sam Menashe, whose fear of women is apparent in his nervousness on entering my room. Seemed to be afraid I might lure him into bed. Absurd, since he actually propositioned me the other night. I think he just likes emoting, revelling in his own mellifluous, dramatic voice. Ricardo V. came too. He has finally been open with me about his homosexuality. And then, Romaine. . . poor angel. Yes, she has caught the crabs.

How shocked she was at first, and then, how tender. She left and came back with ham, tomatoes, oranges, and Sven. Am I in love with her?

It's a rainy, spring day. I think I'll go to work.

EVENING

Went up to the office, but didn't stay. The streets were mobbed with the usual Sunday crowds, and more, brought out by the *beaux temps*. I couldn't stand it.

MARCH 13

Last night I had a talk with Claude. He said, *"Je ne t'ai pas oubliée"* and *"Je t'expliquerais tout ça un jour."* I told him he was always leaving . I called him *"l'homme qui part."* He seemed to recognize that, as though it had been said to him before.

Yesterday was darkened by Irene's letter and her mention of "Nancy," but especially by her wishing me good luck with Romaine. Her lack of jealousy (real?) makes me miserable.

As for me, I got jealous last night when R spoke

to a girl at the party. Jealousy is my weakness. It en-slaves me. I think she is the first really intellectual woman I have ever loved. I am in awe of her, even more than I was of Peggy. She somehow confuses my thinking, and her sexual mastery embarrasses me.

MARCH 15
MORNING

This whole notebook, with all its worrying about whom I love and who loves me, is really dreary.

EVENING

Lately, also, I waste too much time talking to peo-ple who mean nothing to me. Strings of words hang about in my head, and I can't remember who said them, who blew me a kiss. . .

(Just now remembered; it was Dorothy Harvey).

This afternoon, I had a talk with Ida Leach about politics, but her interest in "getting things clear for oneself" seems fairly futile.

Poor Han [van der Ploeg] is reading Howard Fast! He is certainly not enjoying being a Communist. This reminds me of that pathetic, pimply girl at NYU, who wanted me to join the John Reed club and who, when I told her I was going to Black Mountain, said, "Oh, but it's not like it used to be," meaning Stalinist.

MARCH 19

Another miserable night with Romaine. No matter what we do, it doesn't work. This time I didn't come either. I told her it was because I was waiting for her, but that wasn't really true. And the cruel night dropped me, finally, into a heavy, sweaty sleep, a bad sleep, like I always have with her.

She raged about my refusal to go to Lacoste with them and got upset when I suggested I might bring someone with me. She throws these big, jealous scenes when anyone touches me, but sometimes I think it's all theater. The worst moment was her remark as she walked me to the bus stop, "*Peut-être,*"she said, "*je n'ai pas d'amour physique pour toi . .*" Yes, yes, I guess that's it!

MARCH 21 FIRST DAY OF SPRING

A sweet, gray day, long with rain. R phoned last night, but I couldn't speak to her. She called again today, and I felt the same. Hanna thinks that Sven is becoming bitter. She worries about him and says he spends too much time preparing clay for Romaine instead of painting. I think, once again, he is being dominated by a woman, a position that seems natural to him.

MARCH 29, 1956

My 27th birthday came and went, meaninglessly. I spent the night and morning with Romaine. I know that she wants the sex to work as much as I do. She has stopped inventing reasons for our failure. She says, "*Il faut beaucoup de patience.*" We had a lovely breakfast in the sun, grapefruit, croissants and all, and were visited by a ladybug (*coccinelle*). She called it "*la bête de Dieu.*" How strange that at the beginning of an affair, wonders and omens seem to appear everywhere.

And that night, Irene called from Spain. It's awful to recognize how much power she still has over me, and I, perhaps, over her as well.

Then R came yesterday, and left me a letter, the first one I've had from her. She came back today.

EASTER SUNDAY

Feeling lousy all weekend, fearful, lost, alone. Since the other day, when her reckless flirting with me drew such a violent reaction from Sven, I've felt jittery, evil. It's an ugly situation, and, makes me feel ugly too. This morning they were supposed to go to Chartres but missed their train. Sven seemed depressed; she cheerful—she enjoys it! She likes to torment him by referring to things he doesn't *get*. She likes to press my foot under the table.

"Give my regards to God," I said, as they boarded the later train.

This afternoon I went to Notre-Dame with Elliott [Stein]. He talks too much; spoiled my pleasure in being there. Later, in his room, he showed me a horrible sadist magazine that made me feel sick and morbid. That's his thing, apparently.

I am feeling trapped.

MONDAY

Went to the *Préfecture de Police* to renew my work permit, and they turned me down! I suspect this was because of that scene with Algerian Ricardo, witnessed by the boss at the Hôtel de Poitou. He surely reported it. Because of the rebellion, the police are suspicious of anyone involved with an Algerian. I will probably lose my job over this.

Had an erotic letter from Harry.

What a pity that sex with Romaine is no good. That damn French intellectuality! It ruins everything. How I miss the passionate Spanish love language. *"Ay mi vida, entrañas mias!"*

APRIL 5

Woke up to a sore throat, headache, and a dirty gray day, oozing rain. Spent last night with Elaine, an

American lesbian, and some others. How dull it was; what a waste of time.

They just called me to the phone, and it was R, saying she'd like to come over this afternoon. Indifferent. . .

Had a letter from Irene saying, "Come, come. . ." but it was violent and loveless, probably written to bug Nancy. . .Romaine is late, but so what? We're not getting anywhere anyway.

APRIL 12

Totally willful, blind drunkenness brought me to their place this morning, and they both made love to me and I had beautiful orgasms. I think that's what she really wants, a true menage a trois, to have her cake and eat it too.

APRIL 15

Friday night, the three of us went to my room and did it again, and I was too drunk to understand, but somehow it felt as if she loved me.

Had a letter from Irene saying she is coming, and I don't want her to. I am having my usual anxieties, nightmares, in which she gets involved with Romaine!

R called me at work tonight. She sounded very strange. Said she was in Auteuil but didn't want me to come; then suggested Monday. It's pretty obvious she doesn't want to be alone with me. Maybe they have made an agreement that Sven must always be involved. But then she says, "*Tu dois avoir confiance en moi. . .*" But really, how can I trust her?

APRIL 17

They tell me Evelyne [London] is insane. It's too terrible! I keep picturing her in that dark room at the *Hôpital de la Salpêtrière* alone and confused. She doesn't know where she is, or why. I am one of the only people who visited her. Her illness is somehow like a punishment for her ugliness, a terrible vengeance upon her for being unlovable. She must go back to the States!

Silence from Romaine.

I saw Ida Leach today with her new baby, my goddaughter, Anna Francesca Louisa. How blessed is Ida, to be beautiful and loved. When I think of Evelyne, the unfairness of it all really hurts.

Late last night, at the *Bar des États-Unis,* I got up and sang with the piano player, "Yesterdays." I was very happy, wrapped in the music, the brown hands of the pianist, in a New York dream. I wish my sister Bobbie were here. She alone could understand my feelings.

May 1

It's a dark, chilly day. Hardly any *muguets* [lilies of the valley], killed by the cold snap. It's a dead holiday, wilted, without parades.

Friday night with Romaine. . .the bound hands, the pen. . .did she really come? Something has changed; she seems troubled. She actually came to the Bonaparte looking for me. And I seem to be living in one of those Proustian "heart's intermissions," a state of indifference. She phoned yesterday and, for the first time, recklessly left her name with the desk clerk.

God, I'm sick of the stinking job and the lousy life I'm leading! Why do I stay here? I guess I'm waiting for things to take care of themselves. I've always avoided making decisions. Outside of disasters like disease and death, which change everything, you're pretty much on your own.

May 2, Café Terrace

I dare to think R really loves me. She called last night, furious, because I wasn't home when she came over Monday morning. She said, *"Tu l'as fait exprès!"* [You did it on purpose].

Two tall nuns pass by, carrying enormous packages, while I unwrap my *religieuse* (chocolate éclair).

Five old ladies sit on a bench across from the café. Three tiny girls are at a table drinking "Vérigoud" orange sodas. The ladies on the bench lean forward, smiling at a small girl running among the tables. "Christine, Christine!" her mother calls.

The other night, when we got to her apartment, R said, "*Que c'est bien d'être chez nous!*" (How good it is to be in our place!).

MAY 4

I have an idea for a novel about the mother-daughter relationship. . .the daughter who devotes her life to her mother. Ida Leach's friend said, "I finally understand maternal love. I felt it for my own mother. I fed her and combed her hair and did all the other awful things one has to do for a baby." The girl who loves her mother, never marries and withers away. More awful, I think, than the Oedipal scenario.

MAY 6

The affair with Romaine is over. She loves Sven, and I can expect nothing further from her. She writes, "*Je n'ai pas la force pour lutter contre une certaine fatalité . . .*" (I don't have the strength to combat a certain inevitability.)

MAY 8

I just saw Sven in the street. He was obviously not glad to see me. I guess he knows everything now, and mistrusts me. He has probably read my last letter to R, renouncing all of it. Amazing how things have changed. Just a few days ago, I was thinking that she loved me, and I wasn't sure how I felt about her. And now it's finished! It's like a heart attack . . no violence, no argument. . .just a phone call and a letter. But what really happened between Tuesday and Thursday?

NIGHT

The glamorous, white spring night follows me into my dismal room. I saw them! I somehow knew I would and left work early to catch them. She didn't say a word. She froze; looked thinner and pale. Sven was distinctly cool, although we tried to have a light conversation. But I was relieved to see her suffering, a sort of revenge.

Overwhelmed by the end of *Dylan Thomas in America*; his horrible death. In his relationships, he reminds me of Peggy, "the most loveable human being [I've] ever known," who also destroyed anyone who loved her.

MAY 9

Real spring! I am sitting on the *Ile du Vert-Galant*. A young girl passes by in bare feet with a long, silky braid thrown over her bare shoulder. Her whole pink body burns with excitement as she passes the young guys, her eyes hot and dark. Ah, youth! A light river breeze ruffles these pages and caresses my armpits through my loose shirt. The trees ripple; the chestnuts carry white candles.

MAY 12

This morning, I had a long letter from Romaine saying she loves me and making wild accusations of falseness, indifference—even crossed out as if she had thought better of it—a suggestion that I don't want her anymore because I am trying to get back with Sven! How crazy is that! The most disturbing thing about the letter was a loose scrap of paper saying, "*D'abord, Sven est malade.*" What can that mean?

May 14th, Irene's Birthday

It's a beautiful day. The grass in the Luxembourg Gardens is decorated with tiny white daisies and fallen chestnut blossoms. The trees are full of birds;

pigeons, sparrows, blackbirds. It sounds like a pet shop.

Yesterday, I went to the theater with Romaine and her daughter Anne. She is a pale, thin child; wears glasses, serious and sweet. She resembles R but is more like her father, Pierre, whom I've seen in a photo. Sweet and serious, without R's ferocity. Oh Romaine, I love you.

MAY 15

She says Sven knows. She says she loves me. It's clear something awful is going on between them. She came to the Bonaparte. She called me this morning. I ran into Katherine Dudley, who said, "Romaine is so charming," which made me jealous since no one knows of our connection. I wanted to say, "But she loves *me*!"

I bought lilacs. They make a garden of my room.

MAY 20

Is she simply trying to destroy me? She overcomes my reservations, my scruples, and then stays away. Is my surrender all she really wants? Today, I was shocked to learn that she had told Sven about our afternoon at the theater and that he had then told Ida about it, as though something completely natural. I spend hours thinking of ways to hurt her, like buying one of her sculptures and destroying it! She has alienated Sven from me, forced me to choose between them and then betrayed me. And soon, they will go away and leave me alone. This situation somehow reminds me of the fate of poor Charlotte in James's *Golden Bowl,* where the couple triumphs, and she is banished and buried at the end.

I visited Evelyne at the hospital today, bringing her a pack of Gauloises, and she said, "*Les fous ne fument pas.*" (The mad don't smoke).

MAY 24

O the little animals, with their quiet presence! The green-and-red-striped caterpillar I found tangled in my hair, a springtime Medusa. The tiny brown mouse, elegant as a whippet in a medieval tapestry, sitting in the window of the antiques shop like a precious object.

I slept with Nissan last night—poor impotent thing . . . but he is sweet. Lying in his bed this morning, I wrote a letter to Romaine.

I ran into the "psychiatrist" whom I met in the *États-Unis.* He was just back from the Midi—Lacoste, Bonnieux—and had seen Sven in a café. He had asked him "*si'il connaissait une très belle fille qui vivait la-bas dans le temps.*" "Oh, yes," Sven replied; he knew me well.

MAY 30

She avoids me, kept her jacket on the whole time she was here. And then, instead of returning the money I lent her, she sent it in an envelope with Sven. I don't want her leftovers, scraps of her love for Sven and others. I begin to realize there are many others—people she sees occasionally, people in love with her, whom she treats to the same line of jive she gives me. People who don't really matter to her.

Yesterday I visited Raymond [Mason]. His wonderful sculpture is very sexual. He was, as usual, tense when alone with me. Is he reacting to my attraction to him or is he nervously drawn to me?

Oh Romaine, you have injured me. Fragments of our last meeting float around in my head. *"Mais tu as besoin de moi!"* she said furiously. I keep looking at other people's loves, trying to find one like mine. Peggy wrote, "I hope you find your Robin" (*Nightwood*). But she *was* my Robin, the original. Romaine says, *"Mon Harriet, je veux la dire."* (My Harriet, I want to say it.)

JUNE 3

It was a wild weekend, starting Friday night, drunkenly bringing home a boring Arab man. But I needed sex really bad.

Last night, I was at the Bal Montparnasse, dancing. It is amazing that I can dance after my awkward adolescence, when I thought it was not for me. Now, both men and women tell me how well I dance! When the hall was almost empty, in came the Russian, Gleb, a big peasant, with blunt nose and blue Mongolian eyes, heavy, gross, and amusing. I think I met him years ago, with Sven at the Dôme. Valerie had been with me, and Gleb and I'd started necking, and she'd gotten teary and jealous. I think we'd been doing it just to get a rise out of her; she's such a perfect victim. He is really a crude, nasty alcoholic, but I brought him to my little room, and we had lousy sex.

When we woke up in the afternoon, he started vomiting horrible yellow bile into the sink. From his liver, he told me.

When he finally left, he said, "Adieu," referring to a story he had told me about raping German women when he was a soldier in the Soviet army. He said true rape is not what happens in bed but when the man leaves and says "Adieu," dismissing the woman.

What a brute!

JUNE 4

It's a gray, muggy day. I had an awful letter from Irene, worried about how people will react if I come back to Ibiza.

Romaine is gone again.

JUNE 5

I am having one of my hypochondriacal panics; sure I've got it this time. . .TB, like my sister had. I went to the clinic in the rue d'Assas for a fluoroscope.

They saw a shadow on my lung and told me to come back for an x-ray. And then the doctor said to come back in three months. He said, "*Ça a l'air trop fort pour etre quelquechose. Si c'etait le TB vous serez vraiment malade.*" He kept repeating, "*Je m'exprime bien?*" (Do I make myself clear?) Oh yes, angelic doctor, yes, yes. It's just old scar tissue from when I was a child.

JUNE 12

Romaine was here today. Her body is beautiful, those round, white thighs, classical breasts. She has promised Sven there would be no sex between us—so she can keep seeing me, so I can come to Lacoste with them. She says to forget what she is about to say to me. *"S'il n y avait pas Sven, je vivrais avec toi. Je veux que tu saches ça."* (If it weren't for Sven I would live with you. I want you to know that.) Can I really believe that?

JUNE 13

Irene is on her way to Paris.

JUNE 16

Slept with Marc P. last night, after a long, exhausting discussion. He is a darling creature but *"Ça alors, c'est vraiment trop petit!"* if you get my meaning. He has a pretty wild animal's face and a slim, well-made body, but the sex was awful! Like most men, he had a hard-on in the morning and started nudging me, and I just felt like kicking him right out! And then there was a knock at the door. It was the piggish Russian saying he wants me to go away with him somewhere this summer. I am certainly not attracted to the idea. He has a dreary, heavy quality about him, a real turnoff.

Marc gave me his book, *L'Itinéraire,* and reminded me we have a date for Sunday. "No, let's not," I said, *"Ça sera exagérer."* I guess he was hurt by that, but really, what would be the point?

JUNE 17

I feel a growing connection to Europe, am increasingly recognizing that my true home is here. Or is it just the idiots at the *Trib,* as compared to my European friends? The *Trib* is not *my* America, and even among the select group of expats I know here, no one is as wise and interesting as Romaine, for example.

She is a special case, of course. We spent the whole evening together, and she would have stayed longer, but it suddenly seemed hopeless and wrong. So I remembered my date with the Russian in Montparnasse and left.

Today is when Irene is supposed to arrive, but so far, no sign of her. Met Alfred Chester at Amex, a friend of hers from Ibiza. Poor thing, he's really in love with her but can't admit it, and besides, he is queer and unattractive.

JUNE 19

R called me tonight at the office. *"Je pense à toi,"* last words of a loving conversation. Still no sign of Irene. Feeling resentful.

JUNE 20

Last night's dream.

I was being transported to a funeral home, where they would put me out of my misery. Dad was taking me there. They hit you on the head with a mallet, like cattle in an abattoir. The place resembled the funeral parlor where they took my mother. Very dark, with a gleam of daylight at one window. I suddenly changed my mind and decided I really didn't want to die just then, even though my life was miserable. Then Mom replaced me, maimed and fragile, as she really was. Dad seemed to be in charge of the whole thing, stern and forbidding. When I woke up, I thought I could smell death.

SUNDAY, JUNE 24

Spent the day at Versailles with Romaine and her daughter wandering through dark, muddy alleys of sweet-smelling, dripping leaves. Anne is a nervous child, deeply in love with her mother. I flirted with her, trying to make her like me, but no way could I compete. R was being very cool, talking about being there with other women and taunting me with fake jealousy about Gleb.

I met her old mother-in-law, with whom Anne lives. She remarked on how tall I am, saying that I am taller than "Marguerite," who must have been one of R's lovers. Obviously, she understands how things are.

MONDAY

Irene is here and on her way over.

JULY 1

First day of my vacation; it's cold and rainy.

Just back from a meeting with Romaine. No, she doesn't love me. It's all over. I dream of escape from Romaine, Irene, all of this fucked up situation. I should pack a bag and grab a train somewhere, Florence, Amsterdam? But then, wouldn't it really be just as good to take the metro to Montparnasse and get drunk? I'm not sure.

Here is a poem I wrote for her.

Attends, attends, la nuit viendra
La nuit chaleureuse, aimante
Nuit des pins et vignes
Ou loin de la fumée des cigarettes tièdes
On se connaîtra.
Ma solitude! Viens cette nuit
Amene tes etoiles de feu, tes bois sacrées
Et frais.
Chaleur pleurant sur les pierres des villes mortes
J'irais avec toi dans cette nuit lointaine
Par des forêts chuchotantes
Nous ne nous dirions rien.
En plein été la neige

Amie de nos peines
Tombera—chaude, chaude. . .

JULY 6

Sitting on the quay of the *ile St.-Louis*. Irene nestles against me, warm and quiet. Six years ago, I sat here writing a description of Paris, wondering about Sven and what would happen between us. Now, Sven is my enemy, my rival. What a terrible transformation: lover, into friend, into rival. The inevitable change will be into stranger, the most terrible of all.

JULY 12

They are leaving tonight. Again she said she would come, but is an hour late and not yet here. I have never understood why people make appointments only to break them. It was she who insisted, fiercely, that she must see me before they leave—as it has always been she who insisted, fiercely and falsely, at every step of our relationship.

I broke a glass at the Bonaparte last night, and it shocked me. My stomach is upset from all the drinking and my nerves from all the drama.

Irene is being distant. Alfred thinks she is more bothered by the Romaine thing than she admits.

JULY 13

Talk with Irene. Why must she always find complicated explanations for the simplest emotions? It's
obvious that she is upset by my acceptance of Romaine's cruelty, and by my gifts to her, but is too
proud to admit it.

Romaine is gone. Alfred is moving into her room
in Auteuil.

What did Sven mean when he said, "You will have
a nice surprise in a few days?" Is he sending me a
present, or does he mean that Bertus is coming?

JULY 15

In the madness of the *Quatorze,* I ran into Han van
der Ploeg, and we wandered together through the
hilarious crowds. He told me his wife was in the
hospital and asked me to sleep with him. I said no.

Last night he came back to the café and told me
about a girl he was in love with when he was sixteen.
He said her name was Harriet and that I am like her.
Han is very beautiful, tall and slim, with a childish,
pointed face and thick gold hair cut short above blue
eyes.

Walking home, he said, "I want you terribly," and
I said that would cause too many problems.

My scruples are really rather pointless though,

since it's obvious that his marriage is decaying and that he is clearly bored. He will certainly betray her with others. And I do find him extremely beautiful. He wears a gold St. John medal around his neck with a rose engraved on its back. He said, "There aren't enough roses."

Earlier in the night of the *Quatorze,* I was with Irene and Alfred and the Mailers watching the fireworks over the Seine from their hotel balcony. Norman is hostile to me, probably as a rival for Irene, and also because I am much taller than he. Adele is a cow, beautiful but dumb, primitive and defensive.

Yesterday, I worked on the mime film with Alejandro Jodorowsky. My makeup was wonderful. I looked like a sinister goddess. It was a pleasure to follow directions, similar to posing for an artist when you are all external and free inside.

I am planning to go to Italy to dream by the sea and then (ulterior motive) to drop by Lacoste on my way home.

Here is a quote from Sappho's invocation to Aphrodite, my translation from French: "For if now she flees you, soon she will pursue you; if she won't accept your gifts, well, soon she will give some to you, and if she does not love you now, soon she will, whether she wants to or not."

Things with Irene are flat and tasteless.

JULY 25
FIRENZE, ITALY

I have it, what I needed: sun, bright air, happy sounds from the street, freedom!

JULY 27

In the Donatello room of the Palazzo Bargello I found the teenaged David, with his hand on his hip and the saucy hat, whose picture has been hanging in my room all winter. I bought a postcard of a bare-breasted Cretan goddess from the Etruscan museum.

Lucia is here with her wonderful cohort of friends. Yesterday, we took a long walk to Julio's house in San Miniato. He is handsome and aristocratic, but talks too much. The house is lovely—one big square room, with all the comforts—telephone, modern kitchen, shower; all perched up there among the cypresses.

Now, I am also perched, on the roof of the *pensione* in shorts and a shirt, looking across the river at: the yellow American Express building, the brick palace where Leland's bar is, a tall column beyond with a figure on top (must find out who), and people cooling off around its base. At this hour, the river is green. A white cat keeps trying to rub against me. Her coat is dirty; probably full of fleas. On a neighboring roof, there is a sentimental terra cotta figure of a little girl. At its foot, sits a very winning and wistful looking white cat, much prettier than this one.

One of Lucia's friends, Vezio, is a funny, rough-bearded guy with an impressive head on a short muscular body. A satyr. Instant sympathy between us.

The night is so beautiful and I am so horny!

AUGUST 3
PROCCHIO, ISOLA D'ELBA, ITALY

Looking over the ragged heads of an army of sun-flowers marching down to the sea. From up here, I am spared the view of all the tents, campers, and cars on the beach. Only a few tethered sailboats.

My last entry about being horny was dealt with the next-to-last night in Florence when I got very drunk at Vezio's place, the big dentist, Jona, making passes at me while I came on to Vezio. At one point, through my boozy haze, I thought it was going to become a threesome, but Jona gave up. Next morning, I discovered that I had bruises and scratches all over, elbows, thighs, nose! There must have been some crazy action, but I don't remember a thing.

(Of course, nothing will come of it, since his girlfriend is here with him in Elba and I am rooming with Lucia).

AUGUST 7

Terrible heat! Poor Napoleon, stranded here!

Still no word from Paris or Lacoste. Lucia is increasingly depressed and kvetchy, and I keep reminding myself that this is my vacation! Elba is a beautiful place . . . cool, clear sea, soft sky . . .

AUGUST 10
SANT'ANDREA, ELBA

A beautiful place—a few farmhouses, vineyards, haystacks—surrounded by thickly wooded hills. The sea is decorated with bobbing algae of many colors floating in the coves, and nearer shore, there are tall, waving rushes like spiky pennants.

Last night, in bed, Lucia told me the story of Pinocchio. We were a bit high, and I felt like kissing her but only managed to pat her head in a comradely way. She has beautiful pubic hair, tight bronze curls like a Greek statue.

END OF AUGUST
LACOSTE, FRANCE

Time sits all around me here, in the quarry where I lie naked on the warm stone. Carved into the rock face at eye level is a man's name and a date: 1842!

Romaine is heavier, with a demanding belly. Is she pregnant? I knew from the start it was going to be impossible, sleeping in their room, hearing her powerful breathing and the liquid, slapping sound of sex. My hands trembled, and I wanted to kill her. I waited, crying silently, until, hours later, she came to my bed and my fist shot out from the sheets into her face. She got up hurriedly, saying in that special, cold voice, "*Je regrette, je regrette,*" and then something I didn't get.

I went outside, barefoot, into the cold, bright, moonlit road and sat in the center of a field against an old stone wall. It was like being in the navel of the night, weeping and cursing her.

In the morning, she said she didn't understand why I had hit her, denying that they had made love, saying, horribly, "*Mais il n'est pas monté sur moi.*"

In Italian, the word for cunt is "fig."

SEPTEMBER 1
PARIS

I am in the *Hôtel de Poitou* in a large, lovely room. It's raining. The day after I wrote the note in Lacoste, above, we agreed to meet. I waited in the lavender field, lying flat on the ground. She passed by and whistled, and I answered. Then we went to the little pine wood, with the needle bed and stone pillow, where I had rested in the morning. We were alone, naked and happy, and made love. I just found out that Irene had read this diary before I left for Italy, which explains why she didn't write me. And Romaine *did*; I found her note waiting for me here.

SEPTEMBER 6, 1956

Had a long letter from R yesterday, lovingly remembering our encounter in the pine wood. Hopefully, she has changed toward me, because the sex was good—imagining that we could be lovers and not just two people devouring each other.

Paris is rainy and cool, and Irene is warm and sweet. Florence and Elba seem very far away, although it was only two weeks ago.

I keep trying to write at work when I have a free moment, but the stupid bitches who come constantly into our office to gossip, always interrupt. Only my sensitive partner, Louisa Noble, knows how to keep her mouth shut.

The faucet is dripping softly into the sink. Irene is drawing at the table. The damn concierge keeps yelling in the hall, and when she stops, her nasty little dog takes over. I am remembering our sex games yesterday—Irene pretending to tie me to the bed and describing all sorts of things being done to me, ending with a dog licking me, as she herself was so sweetly doing . . .

NOTE TO IRENE: Don't you dare read this notebook, naughty girl!

Remembering R's wildness in the lavender field; how crazy and bright she was! It was our first walk together without Sven . . . I whipped her legs with the tall weeds . . .

SEPTEMBER 11

There have been no more messages from R, except for a small note at the bottom of a postcard from Sven to Alfred about staying in the apartment. They are not returning to Paris for a month or more.

Meantime, I am seeing a lot of Irene, and we're getting along surprisingly well. But sadly, the sex hasn't been that good, after two marvelous years. I don't understand it.

Last night at the Bonaparte, I was surrounded by men—the Cubans, a rather pathetic African, and Paolo, the Italian from last spring, who walked me home and asked if he could sleep over because he was tired and lived far away. When I shut the door in his face, I was pleased with myself for having answered, "because I don't want to" when he asked why not. And I enjoyed the awareness, as I relaxed in my big, lovely room, that I had absolutely meant it. Nice to know I am capable of saying, "No."

Walking down the rue Danton last night, I saw a notice for *Israélites Nord-Africains*, informing them that next Friday, September 14 will be Yom Kippur, and giving the time and location of the Kol Nidre ceremony. I seemed to hear my mother telling me I should go for the peace of her soul. And I will go, and will try to fast, too.

Strolling the quays, browsing the bookstalls, I realize how truly comfortable I now am in Paris. Beside this little river, so small compared to the Hudson of my childhood, I am really at home. A bookseller asked me why I cut my hair and why I am not wearing my nice trousers (Levis). He has watery "let me" eyes, but it is a good feeling, being as visible as I am here. They see me! Although sometimes it's annoying—those wondering, mocking, admiring, disapproving glances—I am seen . . . and it matters!

This is the last page of the red notebook from Barcelona, the book of Romaine.

1:00 A.M.

I am alone in my big bed, missing you, Irene.

Notebook Five

It's a rainy morning and I woke up too early; I hate that! Awful Brahms' Hungarian Dances on the radio. Up since nine; went to the préfecture de police, had coffee and a croissant. Walked in the drizzle and bought this notebook and some red dahlias. A beautiful photo of Ricardo Vigón flirts with me from the mirror.

On the table is a rubber ball I bought in Elba . . . deep blue, with a sunburst design in red and yellow. I bought it for Irene but its colors faded after Lucia, Ernst and I played with it on the beach, so I'm keeping it.

Remembering Lacoste. We lay naked in the garden, flat on our stomachs, our shoulders touching, peering up into the fig tree's big, shapely leaves, watching the kitten.

I've been up and down the stairs. A man in a bathrobe at the hall telephone said, *"Bonjour Mélisande."*

Just now, as I was starting to feel lonely, Irene called. This is the fifth notebook of these diaries. Soon, they will contain ten years of my life . . .

September 16

Last night, we went to the Montagne with an American girl, and as always happens, someone, a French girl, fell in love with Irene, and they danced together all night, leaving me stuck with the American. The French girl was very butch and was treating me like one of the boys, which I hate. I really dislike dykes! When Irene disappeared, I left with the American and, not finding her in the street, choking with rage, said,"They've gone off together!" But then, suddenly, there she was, my little girl in her too-long dress, coming merrily around the corner. Of course, the relief I felt turned immediately into anger, and I slapped her, hard, across the face. Poor baby . . . she really hadn't deserved it. She was furious!

September 17

I am sitting outside the Café de la Palette, still not fully awake. It is a cool, sunny day. The Yom Kippur Kol Nidre service was an incredible spectacle. A continuous quarrel was going on between the rabbi and an officious gentleman in a white satin robe, prayer shawl, and candy box hat, as they stood in front of a makeshift ark, holding the Torah scrolls in their arms. The officious gentleman said, glaring at the congregation, "*Nous sommes trés solennels main-*

tenant" (We are very solemn now) as if we had to be told, and kept interrupting the ceremony every two minutes, until the furious rabbi said, *"C'est moi qui commande ici. Si vous voulez partir, partez!"* (I am in charge here. If you wish to leave, leave!) The shocked congregation tried to calm him down, but he kept shouting, *"Je casse tout!"* (I spoil everything!)

I tried to think of my mother, but that barbarous scene made it impossible.

SEPTEMBER 21

Just had a terrible explosion with Irene, who is in revolt against me. She says I don't question myself enough, that I live in a fantasy of power I don't really possess. She says I took her respect and admiration for granted, although never her love, was what I wanted and felt I never had. Maybe I was wrong . . .

SEPTEMBER 25

Just finished Pavese's novel *La bella estate (The Beautiful Summer)*. Unusual for a man to be so interested in lesbian relationships. (Proust, of course, is the great exception.) Vezio sent me a photo he took of me on the Elba boat, a very interesting portrait in which my eyes are closed. *"Cari salute,"* *(Dear greeting)* she wrote on the back. Now, reading Pavese, I realize that I have always underestimated the Italians; they are much more complicated than I thought.

Things with Irene are very strange. She says we must discipline ourselves to stop seeing each other so often. Alfred thinks she is just now becoming aware of the depth of her need for me and that it frightens her. Or maybe she's just withdrawing from me because she's bored! We took pictures of each other in Ricardo's room; one nude, of me. She looks rather tired and sad in them. She is so much more sophisticated now than when I met her. She says I will be her last female lover. I don't believe it for a minute!

SEPTEMBER 26

I'm trying to write an erotic novel for Olympia Press—calling it *The Virgin*. It's hard to get the right tone. I tend to get too dramatic and personal, and that doesn't work.

OCTOBER 2

Irene left yesterday for London. I miss her already.

OCTOBER 12
PARIS

Got back last night from London: smoky, foul-smelling air, yellow street lamps that turn you into a corpse, enormous crowds in Piccadilly. It's a metropolis, like New York but with occasional quiet pockets, little squares bordered by blank-faced old houses, tiny mews tucked into corners.

Irene seems rather lost there, and needed comfort which I didn't provide. The first night, after dinner at the soup kitchen, walking out into Knightsbridge, she took my arm and leaned her head against my shoulder. She seemed to be about to say something, but stopped herself. Later, when she was mad at me, she said it had been, "I love you."

I wouldn't go with her to the dentist, and she was hurt. But I had so little time there and wanted to reconnect with the London I knew with Sven. I saw Peter de Francia, who was very warm and friendly and asked me to write to him. He also took my Paris address. I really don't know why.

The night before I left, we had hot sex, touched with her hostility and resistance, a struggle that ended in great orgasms for both of us. But I am getting tired of her constant reproaches. Like the day we went shopping and she yelled at me in the street and then broke down in tears over tea at Lyons. I felt absolutely cold, standing there while her sad voice screamed at me and curious crowds swept by. Then she apologized, although she obviously felt I had wronged her.

I can't seem to get anywhere with the porno I'm trying to write. Especially after reading Alfred's *Chariot of Flesh* that we smuggled into London, mine seems tame, unimaginative, puritanical. I just don't seem to have the talent for it.

SATURDAY NIGHT

I'm meeting Alice Jackson and Ricardo at the Bonaparte at 11:30. It feels odd to walk the boulevard Saint-Germain alone at night, but not sad, because Irene will be back soon. What a peculiar life I lead, built on the shifting sands of a girl's love, vague desires (Han), and anticipations (Romaine's return). None of it is the solid stuff of most people's lives: family, work, regular hours, vacations . . .

OCTOBER 15

Well, I finally forced myself to have sex with Alice when she made it impossible to refuse her. The truth is, she rather repels me physically, probably because of her redhead coloring. She's covered with freckles like a spotted animal, leopard or something. Her body is wiry and muscular with a smooth, flat belly, which I don't really like, and that fantastic straw-berry blonde pubic bush, which almost scares me. She wanted to do it again last night, but I rather un-graciously refused. I suspect she's in love with me, which doesn't interest me at all.

Truth is, I really want a MAN!

OCTOBER 16

It's been an awful day, lonely and depressing. I for-got to pay for my coffee at the Mabillon, and the waiter followed me into the street shouting. I lost a thousand francs somewhere and ran into Myriam Plettner, a friend (lover?) of Irene's, and then dreary old Iliazd, who has a crush on her and resents me.

OCTOBER 26

My life with Irene is drawing to a close. In a few days, she moves into her new place, a *chambre de bonne*. It has been good leaving the office at night knowing that the room will be warm and inhabited after the dark indifference of the métro.

OCTOBER 27

I ran into Marc Pierret, who talked about hitchhiking north, giving up the job, and starting another life in a new place among tall Scandinavians. How wonderful it is that there are still so many new places to explore: Vienna, Prague, Moscow, Copenhagen. . . . Travel is such a relief, so liberating: to grow a new skin, new eyes, new ears.

NOVEMBER 6

Election Day in America. Here, a war over Suez seems imminent.

Mad men surely run the world! While the rest of us just want to live, to eat and sleep and work and travel and make love. What happens to us when the leaders drag us into danger for their own selfish, crazy reasons?

NOVEMBER 9

I slept alone last night for the first time in weeks. When I entered the room, I felt sad, but settling down with a book, bread and butter, and a glass of wine I began to enjoy the silence and being truly alone. It was cold in bed, of course, but I had fascinating dreams about Romaine.

Oh, and for the sake of coherence in these pages, I should mention that Britain and France have dropped their plan to attack Egypt, so the war is not on for this week.

NOVEMBER 20

Sleeping alone is hard. Last night, I kept channeling Irene, as though I were inside her head. I imagined her going to Diorka, asking him to rescue her from the terrible emptiness in her life. Or deciding to return to the States to escape from it. Is this inevitable in lesbian relationships; this fear of time passing, of being shut away from real life? Or is this just the way I feel about it? But then, my sister's letter of yesterday describes her relationship with Brendan as just as futile and crippling as any lesbian one.

Irene told me the other day about her older brother who molested her for years, starting when she was nine, and of her silence, which he took as a sign of complicity. She remembered being in the subway with him when she was seventeen and he already married and him saying, "You know, we are both outlaws." She'd never told me about this before. Was it that memory that got her so excited she started making love to me although I was fast asleep?

I am feeling a weight of guilt for indefinable crimes against my mother, my sister, my father, Irene, Sven . . .

She just came over, and I see that last night's

thoughts were all my own. Far from being troubled, she was out dancing!

November 23

It is cold; ice in the street. Feeling strangely solitary, turned inward. The French have a word for it, *recueillement*, collecting oneself.

I got an odd surprise the other evening. I've been feeling very jealous of Paola, Irene's Italian friend, but Irene said suddenly, "Well, I just have to tell you. Paola told me she is so in love with you [me!] that she can't even talk to you!"

Last night we made love, and I had odd negative feelings about it, was even slightly repelled, so I couldn't come and she was hurt and angry.

I had a letter from Dad in response to a photo I sent him of me with Ricardo. "Your friend looks nice, but isn't he a bit young?" Beautiful *maricón*! Can't really fool Daddy, can I?

And Romaine? Not a word for months.

November 24

A letter from Sven telling me they are buying a big farm and selling the old house. I immediately thought of buying it myself, but he would certainly not want that, and it would be painful for us both.

DECEMBER 3

I slept with Paola. She has already been with Irene and told her the next day that she was in love with me. But I really don't care.

DECEMBER 5

Things are at a standstill. We separated over a petty argument.

I got up at noon and went out walking, following the quays to the Café Voltaire, where Romaine and I had sat one night last summer. I was alone on the terrace, looking out at the gray bridge and leafless black trees.

December 12 is the second anniversary of my mother's death.

Just got home and she's not here. She met Paola today and is probably in bed with her. It is certainly partly my fault, having said something unnecessary and hurtful to her today, "Romaine is the most exciting woman I know." How stupid of me! It may be true, but Irene is so much more necessary to me, a part of my life.

DECEMBER 11

I have just spent three horrible days, and this notebook is partly to blame. Irene has been reading it and been wounded by it. Three days of running around like a lost dog, climbing the six flights of stairs to her *chambre de bonne*, banging on her door, running home to lie paralyzed on my bed, weeping.

Last night she slept here—no sex, just the comfort of holding her in my arms—but today was bittersweet again. I went with her to meet her brief love of last summer, Barbara, unattractive but intelligent. I tried to monopolize the conversation, to show the girl what she would be up against in a fight for Irene. Sweating and shaking in my parka, I tried to impress her.

I will never give Irene up to another woman. If it were a man who loved her, I would feel criminal if I tried to hold on to her. Double standard indeed!

DECEMBER 12

Two years ago on this date my mother died.

Now, I am waiting for Irene. She said she would come at three; it's twenty to four.

DECEMBER 17

It's my first night alone since our reconciliation. She has been loving and tender for the past few days, but this morning, we had a silly argument about *blintzes*!

Then she brought up my journals again, asked, "Is that fucking thing still lying around?" Diorka is back on her case, but she does seem sincere in her rejection of him. Sunday was a wonderful day; we made love twice. She has a way of covering you with love; making you feel you will never be lonely again.

DECEMBER 23

Her mother, Carmen, arrived last night, and Irene is mad with worry that she will suspect her of being queer. Things are going to be very uneasy during her stay. Last night, I sat with them for hours in a café, while Carmen talked on and on, telling stories. I was feeling trapped, the way I used to be when I had to spend an evening with my own mother. After she took momma to the hotel, she was going to come here. I hung around the cafés to calm my nerves, and when I got home, slightly tight, I made wild love to her. But after she came, she turned away from me in the bed, without a word.

I asked her what was wrong, and she said she had dozed off and that when she'd awakened in my arms, she had thought I was her mother! When I tried to shake her out of her dream-guilt, she accused me of only worrying about my own: "little ego."

When she left this morning, with wide, sad eyes, she asked me if I would try not to resent her mother. Her blindness to my feelings amazed me, because she's always been so good at reading them. I guess there's nothing I can do about her guilt; she'll just have to work it out for herself.

This afternoon I met Han, his wife, and his ex-girlfriend Nora at the Old Navy. Ricardo was there too, and he told Han that I was interested in a job at UNESCO where Han works. Odd, that Ricardo hadn't mentioned it to me before. He is very hostile to the idea of a relationship between Han and me. Whenever we speak of Han, Ricardo asks if I've slept with him and always exclaims, "But he's married!" Too bad I haven't yet. I wonder if he is hot for Han, himself . . .

JANUARY 4, 1957

Irene left for Spain yesterday with Carmen, who has been growing increasingly suspicious and hostile toward me. It's funny and sad that I am being blamed for Irene's homosexuality when she is much more that way than I am. After all, she was the initiator of our relationship.

I am starting to think about moving back to the States if Irene goes. Not an appealing prospect. But my early years here were so much richer. What blights everything now is the fucking job, but what would I do without it?

JANUARY 6

The theme from the movie, *The High and the Mighty* is playing on the radio. I saw it in Miami with Mom and Dad. It was the last film I would ever see with her.

I flew to New York that night, and then to Provincetown to be with my love, and then to Paris. When I next saw my mother, she was mute and half-blind. Whenever I hear that music, I feel her sitting next to me, the warmth of her ailing body. And then, I think of waving goodbye at the airport.

JANUARY 8

I had an awfully nervous lunch with Han at UNESCO.

I think the story I tell Dorothea, my new office mate at the *Trib*, is actually becoming true. I am tired of hiding the gender of my lover. I need a new one that I can show to the world.

NIGHT

I don't know if this is a positive or negative development. For one thing, I no longer feel compelled to go to the Bonaparte. When I left work at midnight just now, I went to the Deux Magots, enjoying the old-fashioned luxury and quietness of it. On my way home, passing the Bonaparte, I saw Jean-Claude Meurice, beautiful and bored as always, leaning against the bar, and was relieved to not have to go in. Lately, too, I seriously avoid male glances on the street. Is this maturity or regression to my adolescent shyness? In any case, the hunger and recklessness of last year now seem unnatural to me, a pose.

I'm reading Camus's *L'homme révolté,* about love:

Nous désirons que l'amour dure et nous savons qu'il ne dure pas. Un matin, après tant
de désespoir, une irrépressible envie de vivre
nous annoncera que tout est fini et que la
souffrance n'a pas plus de sens que le
Bonheur. Le goût de la possession est á ce
point insatiable qu'il peut survivre á l'amour
même . Á la limite, tout homme dévoré par le
désir éperdu de durer et de posséder souhaite
aux êtres qu'il a aimés la sterilité ou la mort.

I translate: We want love to last, and we know it doesn't. One morning, after so much despair, an irrepressible desire to live tells us that it's all over and that our pain made no more sense than our joy. The need for possession is so insatiable that it can last longer than the love itself. In the end, one who is devoured by the mad desire for duration and possession wishes sterility or death on those he has loved.

JANUARY 14, 1957

Spent Saturday night and all day Sunday in bed with Paola. She is just a toy one would quickly tire of. It would not be a good idea to pursue this. She is a hungry girl, and hungry people, especially young ones, can be dangerous, without burdensome scruples. (She took photos of me in bed. Not a good idea.)

JANUARY 16

Had lunch at UNESCO with Ricardo and Han. Han is very polite and very "nice." There is so much unsayable between us. For example, I could never tell a man who is married and whose feelings toward me are so strained, "I want to have a child by you."

JANUARY 18

I slept with Paola again, and it's just no good. I get a kick out of making her come, but she can't do anything for me. She makes me feel like a man. I hate that! Had a nightmare a few days ago in which I was growing penises, not just between my legs, but in my armpits! I woke up terrified, almost determined never to have sex with a woman again!

Alfred got a letter from Sven saying they are staying on in Lacoste, so he can keep the apartment a while longer. I don't understand their life there. Obviously I didn't, or I would still be with Sven.

JANUARY 28

A wild, gray day after a calm sunny week. I have a new bicycle! Lovely to ride along with the wind!

Irene got back a day early and found me in bed with Paola. She sulked for a while but now seems to have forgotten about it.

I've been writing a story about Romaine's daughter, Anne. I gave it to Alfred to read, and he criticized it harshly. He is working on his new novel and doesn't want to see anyone.

We talk on the phone. He likes that because he can get the gossip without having to leave his place.

At yesterday's *vernissage* (gallery opening), there were all the old faces: Hanna and Reggie, Geula, Shamai, and so on. I felt a certain nostalgia for the days when Sven and I were part of the art crowd. Quarreled with Irene because I wanted to leave but she was having fun, flirting with people.

The Paola affair has dwindled away, as it should have. But I did sleep with her, once, since Irene's return, and have kept it a secret. This makes me uncomfortable. I am a lousy secret-keeper.

FEBRUARY 13

Sven's letter today had a little note enclosed from Romaine, "*Je ne sais pas écrire de petites choses*," and then an invitation, seconded by Sven, to come to Lacoste. She adds, "*Avec une amie ou deux amies ou seule, si tu voudras.*" I'm sure she wrote that in reaction to my mention of "friends" in my last letter. It probably also reassures Sven as a suggestion that I no longer want her. I've read her note over and over looking for a hidden word that says "I love you."

FEBRUARY 15

The invitation to Lacoste troubles me. I asked Irene if she wanted to come, and she decided not. This is probably good, since all of us together in that small house would inevitably lead to disaster.

FEBRUARY 24

I stupidly told Irene my little secret (about Paola). She is very upset; Paola too. You'd think I'd know by now, 'what they don't know can't hurt them.'

Irene seems increasingly worried about my visit to Lacoste. Paola advises me not to go.

FEBRUARY 23

Last night while I was writing, I stopped to go to the john, and had a feeling that I should put away this notebook, but I didn't. When I got back Irene was here! Ouch!

I just had lunch at the Arts, and Iris Owens, who writes porn under the name Harriet Daimler, came in and sat at my table. Strangely, she ordered the same thing I had. For some reason, she made me nervous. As she was leaving, she said, "Hello, Harriet," and I pretended I didn't know who she was. Really weird. Then she sat down again and we talked. She told me about her new novel, etc. She is attractive—reminds me a bit of my old professor, Sarah Zweig—but I feel ill at ease with her. Maybe that's because I've read her novel, *Darling*, and feel as though I have watched her in bed. Or else, I sense she's heard rumors about me—that I sleep with men, women, dogs or whatever—and is curious.

ASH WEDNESDAY

Mardi Gras last night. The streets were full of drag queens from the club, Madame Arthur. I felt a momentary attraction to one of them, but only because he reminded me that under the long red wig and the falsies, he was a man! He asked me if I had ever slept with a man, assuming I was a dyke! Of course, he wasn't serious, but all my recent brooding about sexual identity was somehow relieved by my encounter with the *travesties*. With them, I felt very much a woman—my severe butch outfit being a sign of my femaleness, since they dress in that exaggeratedly feminine way.

Irene and I roamed around with them the whole night. They played cruel games with the workmen at Les Halles, scaring a poor, frightened boy, who spilled a crate of cabbages from his wagon at the sight of them.

We slept late and made beautiful love, better than we have for a long time.

MARCH 20

I saw Alice Jackson tonight, her last in Paris. We talked about New York and the crowd—Peggy, Blanche, glamorous Natika whom I've never met. She seemed worried about an affair she'd had in Italy and referred to her "real life" in New York—those hot summer nights, missing them. I know! I do, too! I felt I had to explain to her why I live here and not there. But in a way, I am starting to feel that Europe for me is something like homosexuality—a fantastically exciting detour, an unforgettable addiction— but not real.

MARCH 27, 1957

Yesterday was my twenty-eighth birthday. I seem to be rushing toward that age when everything will be fixed, settled, without having achieved any of my goals . . . writing, publishing, marrying, bearing children. How dreadful!

Irene's affair with Paola's lover, Wanda, has upset me. "Do you think you still love me?" she asked, when I wept. I answered, "I know I do." Yet she administers large doses of poison. Tonight, after calling me at the office and asking me to meet her, she has stood me up. The first time in all these years, she has actually done that! There is a heavy, drawing sensation in my pelvis. Could it be another dose of the clap? *Quel horreur!*

I leave for Lacoste next week. My nerves are shot. Seems as though the older I get, the weaker I become. I cry a lot, feel sorry for myself.

APRIL 9
LACOSTE

It's over, a week down the drain! Just shreds of memory in my sick head!

Lying in bed with Romaine; my cold feet between her thighs. My period, a painful one. Sven's repellent kisses; his bad breath; his fat tongue, forcing. Our sexual incompatibility . . . no wonder; no wonder I never enjoyed it. And his desperately insecure personality; how he sucks up to strangers at the expense of whoever is close to him. He flirted with Rachel Jacobs; ignoring Romaine and me. It was infuriating! I think it annoyed her too. It's strange that I never recognized what made him so awful when other people were around. Pathetic.

APRIL 10
PARIS

I have to write something about the boy on the train from Marseille. He was blond and red-faced, with one mangled ear and one pushed-in blue eye. Early in the trip, I noticed him staring at me in the corridor, wearing dark glasses and smoking dramatically. When we reached Lyon, he moved into my compartment. I left my seat, while he settled in with his dirty canvas sack, cardboard suitcase, and guitar wrapped in brown paper. When I returned, he had begun chatting with the other passengers in a peculiar French, all infinitives and objective pronouns, *"Moi venir Indochine, moi chanter cabarets, Nice, Cannes, fait beaux temps ici . . . "* (Me come Indochina; me sing in clubs, Nice, Cannes, nice weather here), waving his big red hands.

I knew at once that the boy, with his Midi accent, was pretending to be a foreigner. But the others in the compartment didn't seem to get it, and were transfixed with curiosity. After the stuff about being a singer in nightclubs, he proceeded to recount his whole life story. He said he had been born in Indochina, with a father who was a sea captain. His mother had died when he was little, he said, and his father had been tortured to death by the Russians. He gave detailed descriptions of the torture—tearing out of fingernails, teeth, etc.—making the old ladies scream.

Then, he described his life in Saigon living with a wealthy family. He said that his Chinese driver, who had followed him from Saigon, had refused to come to Paris. "*Moi furieux. Moi presque tuer chauffeur.*" (Me furious. Me nearly kill chauffeur). The car, he said, was worth three million francs. I was dismayed at the boy's lies, some of which were extremely grotesque and designed to shock. For example, stuff about cooking and eating habits in China. At the same time, I felt a sort of satisfaction at seeing these French bourgeois being taken for a ride. But the most puzzling part of it to me was their acceptance of his peculiar speech and treatment of him as a foreigner. To embellish his impersonation, he would frequently pretend not to know simple French words, like *frère* and *valet*.

Back to Lacoste. I had a strange conversation with Sven about my desire to have a child. He offered to give me one if I really wanted it. But how ridiculous would that be, having never thought of it when we lived together?

Irene has gone to Italy to see Wanda.

I saw Algerian Ricardo last night as I passed the Bonaparte. He beckoned to me to come in, but I kept on going.

APRIL 11

Morning coffee at La Palette. The café is full of characters today. The man next to me just anxiously asked for a *café crème* and then changed his order to a glass of warm milk and sugar, no coffee. He looked like someone who had spent a long time in a hospital; he has that cringing demeanor that such people develop. He talks softly to himself.

Now the students are piling in for their noon coffees. *Je file!* I'm outta here!

SUNDAY MORNING

Eleven-thirty, still in bed, drinking Nescafé, alone, but not lonely.

Last night, Paola and the other Italian girl stood me up. Alfred said, "Well, if they don't mean anything to you, what does it matter?" Darling Alfred;

he's always so sensible about other people's problems. But it wasn't that I missed them; I missed dancing with girls in bars. I'd been looking forward to it . . .

So I threw myself on the mercy of the night, and who should appear but Ricardo Vigón, just back from Ibiza. We sat at the Flore for a while and then took a cab to see *Anna Karenina* with Garbo. There were no seats, and we had to stand close to the screen, and her enormous, heavenly face started to blur before my eyes. I stumbled through miles of people, feeling ill and faint, and sat down on a bench in the lobby. When I went back in, I found a seat. The film is great. I especially love the train scenes, like the one where Vronsky and Anna are on the same train to St. Petersburg, and you see them both at dawn, looking out from separate windows at the mountains.

Only a week ago, I lay in bed with Romaine, the sun pouring over our faces. Then Sven stuck his head in at the door. Oddly, twice, when I was about to have a marvelous orgasm with him going down on me, we were interrupted by noise, or the taxi come to take me to Aix, and he stopped abruptly. It almost seemed deliberate, as if he were punishing me.

SUNDAY NIGHT
PARIS, ALONE . . .

The other night, I had a dream about making it with that guy Kelley from the *Trib* office. A real fuck! Even in my sleep, I felt my vagina open to let him in. It's sad that I waited so long to lose my virginity and then had the bad luck to do it with Sven, a man who could not satisfy me. I wasted three and a half years with him and women, until Peter F. finally gave me the real thing in New York. How sad it is to be in this great, beautiful city without a man to fuck!

APRIL 18

The medieval French songs on the radio just now reminded me of Romaine and that August afternoon in the yellow field when she sang to me, "Le roi renaud" and a sea chantey, "Pique la baleine" . . .

Alfred told me last night that Irene said she'd be gone for two or three weeks. For some strange reason that comforts me, I feel that she won't stay away longer because she's in love.

Went to a piano recital by Alfred's lover, Arthur. He looks very beautiful when he performs. One could fall in love with him, only then..

APRIL 24
ILE DU VERT-GALANT

Still no letter from Irene or Romaine.

It's a marvelous, warm spring day. The quays are crowded with English and German tourists. Groups of workmen in blue denim are eating their lunches on the parapet. I ran into Han the other day, and we had our usual teasing conversation. I really must sleep with him—it's spring; Irene is away; his wife is away too. He said, "Some people at UNESCO thought you were my wife."

APRIL 25

I spat blood this morning. That old devil TB is still on my trail. X-ray tomorrow. Results on Monday. Maybe it has finally caught up with me. Now there's a "secure torment" for you, much stronger than the one in *Nightwood*. If it's real, it will be sort of a revolt against this ridiculous life I'm living.

MAY 1

Han and I finally made it . . . not great sex, I'm afraid, but nice being in bed with someone I like.

Irene arrived soon after he left for work. We made wonderful love but my body kept remembering last night, comparing what D.H. Lawrence called "the fine white ecstasy" of a clitoral orgasm to the deep soul-warming comfort of the vaginal. More and more, I prefer it to that sharp, thin joy.

Well, the x-ray was OK, and I am back to being selfish and tormented, instead of being grateful. I had promised myself I would change if I escaped again, but no; I am still who I am!

MAY 5

Back in the empty darkness. Han rejects me (of course), and Irene is busy, distant, friendly. I told her something I shouldn't have, that I am too dependent on her and am longing for someone new to release me. She was annoyed.

MAY 12

I have this notebook here in the office. Have to keep it away from her. I saw Han this afternoon at the Tournon with Iris Owens, that bitch! Mean of him to go there when he knows I always do on Sunday afternoons.

MAY 19

This afternoon, I put on a sheer pink nightgown that Mother gave me years ago. Looking at myself in the mirror, I saw a beautiful woman with delicate, round breasts, erect nipples and long, soft, dark hair. It made me imagine a different life for myself, in which

I always wore luxurious materials, silks and velvets, instead of the denim, leather, and boots I wear now. I am tired of this persona. Could I transform myself?

MAY 22

Oh, I hate coming back to an empty room where I have made love and facing the unmade bed. Looking at Irene's adorable photo on the mirror, I already can feel the pain I will suffer when she leaves Paris.

Today, we talked about the future, and she said she wants to get married and have children. Of course, she will, since she always gets what she desires. While I imagine myself going down into solitude, illness, old age. . . . Most of all, I hate it when she comforts me, a display of her strength and my weakness. Am I being ungenerous?

JUNE 7

Another betrayal, with a sixteen-year old girl! And she laughed, telling me what happened at the party: "I was drunk, leaning against the wall. I said, '*Embrasse-moi,*' and that was all I had to do!" Reminds me of Peggy! Haven't I sworn never to love another Dona Juana!

JUNE 8

A distraction from my misery. Harry Bell is here, and seems to want to resume our affair, but I don't really believe it. I think it's all in his head, his memory of the mad, brief passion he felt for me in New York. I don't really want him, but I suppose we will have to make it. Feels like an obligation.

JUNE 24

Slept with Harry last night . . . what a mistake! The five minutes of pleasure, I paid for with all that awkwardness, embarrassment, and those *bad smells*! What is wrong with his stomach? And the frantic boredom of our conversation!

JULY 5

It's a hot, hot day, so rare in Paris. I stay home, contentedly naked in the darkened room, listening to Bach on the radio. I do love the heat; it lets you go nearly nude in the streets, like they do in Miami but hardly ever do here.

Painters are hanging on scaffolds just outside my window. I wickedly imagine their reactions if I suddenly pulled open the curtains. Who would be the more excited? Embarrassed?

The U.S. just exploded the most terrible bomb yet. The radio says it shook the earth and made a *"fracas terrifiant!"* Bravo! *Vive les Américains!* What a disgrace!

This morning, when I came back from the john, Irene was lying naked on the bed with her eyes shut. Hearing me, she tried feebly to pull the sheet over herself. Her very short hair, recently cut, matches the little pubic cap that accents the round forms of her lush body. I speak and she smiles, still without opening her eyes.

JULY 8

Next week, I travel south and she north. How nasty she was when she came back to her room and found me there! Saying I was reading her letters! And how many times has she peeked into these diaries? I hadn't even thought of her fucking letters. How petty and ugly she can be. I rode away on my bike without a word.

JULY 19
TY MEN, A HOUSE IN BRITTANY

I'm here with Harry, visiting his friends the Hays. It's a wild place—old castles, rain and sea, odd names.

What a pity I'm not in love with him! If I were, our stolen encounters, absent from excursions, meals, would be delicious. Last night, lying by the fire in the big, beautiful salon with its doors open to the stone terrace and the stormy sea—how magnificent it would be with someone I loved!

JULY 23
NANTES

Hitchhiking alone on my voyage south. So far, no problems, just a close call with a red-haired man from Vannes, who stopped on a bright hilltop on the way here and asked for *"Juste un petit baiser,"* with his hand stroking the side of my so-soft cashmere sweater.

Just a little kiss, and I'll take you all the way to Nantes. First, he'd said he'd take me to the *"prochain village."* When I still refused, he drove off and then came back, got more insistent, stopped his car right in the middle of the road, pleading, increasingly urgent and embarrassed. And then, along came my rescuer, a small, young, dark truck-driver whom I desperately thumbed down, not really expecting the beat-up old truck to stop.

I got in, and he asked if I would mind waiting a minute while he picked some flowers. I said, "of course," thinking he was going to pee, but he actually returned with wild flowers and added them to a pretty little glass vase attached to the dashboard.

Now, I am sitting in a fairly expensive restaurant, after having registered at the youth hostel. I'm awfully tired; brain functioning poorly. Well, here's the bill; maybe I'll go and look at the cathedral.

LATER

The church and the Château des Ducs de Bretagne are lovely, but this town seems to be full of cretins— young ones, old ones—like the idiot on a bicycle, staring open-mouthed at me while I sit here at the café. I've been followed till I can't take it any more. Heading back to the hostel. The waiter just angrily brought me a glass of water!

SUNDAY, JULY 28
LACOSTE, VAUCLUSE

Since I arrived on Friday, we have celebrated our little ritual twice a day, but only just now did I manage to make Romaine come and to orgasm myself with Sven. Until now I've just been bored and resentful.

My feelings for her are wildly ambivalent. Sometimes I actually find her repulsive, with her vicious side like Harry's. Then again, she can be lovely and delicate.

Now, I hear them coming up the stairs. What am I

doing here? Really, in some ways, Brittany was better, especially the food; the wonderful butter, juicy meat, fine young carrots and radishes. Here, I am mightily sick of Sven's eternal ratatouille!

AUGUST 4

R's behavior toward me is bizarre. Last night, as we were dressing to go into the village, she opened her legs to me. A few days ago, we agreed that she and I would sleep together with S in the other room. But when we began making love, he stormed in wanting to join us and I left the room. Since then, there's been no sex at all.

New guests are arriving today, including John Berger, the famous writer and art critic. Romaine made a drawing of Sven and me fucking.

AUGUST 5

I am in the cave where, last year, I wrote our initials in a heart on the wall and they are still there. Right now, I hate her again, how she derails my feelings, confuses my desires with false clues. And she admits doing it!

The cave walls are covered with crude, illiterate graffiti. "*Furee un con ses pas lapene*" (Digging into a cunt is not worth the effort) and, by the same hand, "*Vive amour ses con*" (Long live love is stupid). Another wrote, "*Quand tu le mettras reste y longtemps*" (When you put it in, stay there a while). Another, or is it the same sex rebel as above: "*La Madelon avec ses gros nichons et avec ses grosse couilles*" (Madelon, with her big tits and big balls)?

There is an atmosphere of pagan ritual in the cave, and it smells of shit. Just now, when I went deeper, a crowd of furiously buzzing black flies rose up around me. The guardians of the cave! One more, "*Le vier est le plus bel instrument de l'homme*" (The cock is man's most beautiful tool), accompanied by a chalk drawing of that very thing. And another, with a picture of a prick entering an anus, "*Vive la Madelon qui tranche la couille de Napoleon,*" (Long live Madelon who fucks Napoleon's ass). And more, "*Va te faire tranche avec une chevre*" (Get fucked by a goat). Near the cave's entrance is written in large letters: "ATTENTION; DANGER DE MORT." What wild peasants are here in the wild Vaucluse! The old Marquis de Sade knew what he was doing when he built his château in Lacoste!

AUGUST 13

How should I interpret her attitude these last few days? Remarks: "When will we travel together?",

"Hitchhiking would be fun with you." And this morning, "I need to be alone with you; otherwise my life becomes . . . " interrupted by tears. Her beautiful gray-blue-green eyes on me at lunch.

Day after tomorrow, I leave for Venice and Irene.

AUGUST 1957
SALERNO, ITALY

This is the end. I will return to Paris alone, while she stays here with someone else. After three years of her obsession with me, it's finally really over. Our other breakups were angry and passionate; this time is different. We are alone in Alfred's house, a beautiful old place on a hill above the sea. Alfred will arrive soon. How odd it is that, when Alfred left Paris, I felt he was taking the last scraps of Irene's love with him, and now the end will come in his presence. Strangely, in spite of all this, we had great sex today in the sun.

SEPTEMBER 1

Reading in the grape arbor. Arthur, Alfred's lover, plays the same tunes over and over on the piano. Maddening. . . . Irene sits farther down the slope, drawing, her little face screwed up against the brightness. I have my period.

SEPTEMBER 3

Coming to the end. The thought of returning alone to Paris makes me dizzy. It's a sad, grey day, with grey sounds from the piano. I am in pain.

SEPTEMBER 23
PARIS

Alfred kicked us out of San Marco because Arthur objected to our presence while he practiced for his concert. We had to hitchhike back to Paris together. It was almost as if they understood my predicament and decided to end the dark, suicidal ordeal in which I was submerged. What unexpected grace! We had a happy day in Rome and on the beach at Ostia, and a lovely night in Florence, and then back to Paris, together!

But the end is approaching.

NIGHT

Sat in a café with Roger Blin. How tense he is! I said to him, "*Vous êtres très inquiet ce soir, non?*." He said he was just tired. I wonder why someone so beautiful and famous seems so alone and sad. And what can one do with a man who never says "stay" or "*à bientôt*" but who just gives you his delicate white hand

and says, "*Au revoir.*"

Silent meetings may speak more than conversations.

A handshake may be warmer than a bed.

Who will the night bring to dress me in silver with a breath?

Our love is sick and dying.

The pictures on my walls are all of you, but they have no eyes.

There is no one here but you, and you are gone.

SEPTEMBER 26

Just ran into Han's friend, Nora. She says that he and Iris are through. I got a sad, sour-grapes kind of satisfaction from that. She says that his wife, Monique, is more important to him than any other woman.

OCTOBER 10

It really is the end. Irene and I are no longer lovers. Can we be friends? I think not. Will she leave Paris? Probably not; she just wanted to end things between us. All our previous breakups were avoided by my refusal to accept them. Now, I have to; can't take any more pain.

She said, "We are not in love any longer," and I

said, "Not true; I am still in love with you." But is that so? I'm not sure; I really don't know.

OCTOBER 11

Bad, long, sleepless night. I'm at the café; it's almost noon. My eyes burn.

OCTOBER 24

A deaf-mute day, muffled in solitude.

Harry is a help, but like a bad-tasting medicine that you take because it's supposed to do you good. Sex with him begins well, but then it goes on too long, and my box gets sore, but he just keeps on and starts to sweat. Sven used to do that too. Very disagreeable. Why does he do it? It must be a sign of weakness.

I walk through the ancient streets—Saint Julien-le-Pauvre, rue des Carmes—up to the Pantheon. How dilapidated and sad are these hilly streets. I'd love to go away somewhere, maybe Dublin—my sister is there—or Rome in the sun.

> Oh creature of solitude,
> muffled streets
> unloved and lonely

in a world of lovers
The circling leaves drop on her
as though she were dead.

OCTOBER 29

I must get rid of these sick habits, like still being jealous, when it is absurd now as things are. And brooding about moments, like two weeks ago, when I modeled the fur jacket for her and she kept playing with my breasts. Just two weeks ago.

I attacked her on Saturday night. Our meetings are disasters. We shouldn't see each other at all, but she keeps insisting; she likes being with me; she still cares about me, etc.

Fuck that shit!

I'm reading Françoise Sagan's book, *Dans un mois, dans un an.* It's not a novel but a series of reflections on love. Some are totally unconvincing; others are horribly poignant like the one about the man calling his love at four a.m. and another man answering the phone. Or the awful situation in which the girl he loves comes to him unexpectedly, to tell him that his wife is having a miscarriage, and he is joyfully surprised by her arrival.

"*Un jour, sans doute, elle se trompera comme lui, et comme lui, elle jouerait au bonheur avec un faux parte-naire.*" (One day, no doubt, she will make the same mistake that he did and will play at joy with a false partner.)

Another man realizes that the woman he loves has never loved him. He gets a certain bitter satisfaction out of thinking, *"Elle ne pourra jamais me dire qu'elle ne m'aime plus."* (She will never be able to tell me she no longer loves me).

The dumb guy at the office who has a crush on me said, as I got out of his car on my way to a café, "Now don't get into any trouble. I know you're unhappy." How does he know that? How does anyone know? But they all do. Except for the Cuban guy in the Bonaparte, who just now called out, gaily, "Where's Irene?"

I'm remembering that horrible night in San Marco, when I tried to open that drawer with the revolver in it but it was locked. Anyway, I was probably too scared. It was a windy night, and the oil lamps were flickering. She said, "I haven't been in love with you for a long time. It's been dying almost since the beginning." I said she was lying, and later she admitted it, but maybe it was only to calm me down. How do you know when you are loved? It's already so hard to know when you love!

OCTOBER 30

I once said to her, "I will not put my life into your careless little hands," and then I did just that! Now,

I have no one to blame for my pain but myself. I walked into it and now must crawl out of it on all fours.

NOVEMBER 22

She is gone. Her ship docks in New York in three days. I've taken over her *chambre de bonne,* which I always hated when it was hers but love now that it's mine. The night before her departure, there was a wild party with much dancing and roaming around. It ended here, in this room, where my hair caught fire from the alcohol lamp as we were making *vin chaud.* I didn't move, though I felt the heat at the back of my head, and covered my face with my hands. It was just an accident, but it was as if I had wanted it, a fire to burn away the pain of losing her at last.

After that (the atrocious smell of burnt hair), I broke down and screamed and cried. She sat there and didn't speak, and everyone just watched me as if I were performing in a play.

I have had two letters from her, mailed at South-ampton and Cobh. I was happy about them, until I ran into that filthy little doll, Gilles, who said she had received a letter too.

December 7

The rain is streaming down my skylight. I am happy alone in this little room. Another letter from her saying she won't be coming back any time soon. Last night I went to the Club Saint-Germain to hear Miles Davis, and I was feeling good alone with the music. That musician friend of Buddy [Wirtschafter] arrived with his poor French wife, who has lost all her teeth. He was charming and cool in that junky style. Reminiscing about Buddy, Charlie Leeds, Miles F., and being in the old NY atmosphere was good. Got home at three a.m., high on music and memories.

I must be careful not to repeat evenings like last Saturday when I hung out with Paolo, Bruno (a gay male hustler), and Gilles and ended up in bed with Bruno. Poor thing; he has the smallest cock I've ever seen! Couldn't feel a thing! He is living off a rich old man, who must enjoy being seen with such a handsome young Italian. He certainly could never satisfy a woman!

Susan Sontag is coming to Paris next week. I'm not sure that I want to see her.

[Susan and I met in Berkeley where she, a sixteen year old prodigy, was taking classes. I was in my junior year at the U. of C., working in a bookstore and in love with Peggy Tolk-Watkins, my first lesbian lover. She had a nightclub in Sausalito called The Tin Angel. Susan and I became friends, and I initiated her into the world of women lovers, to which she was extremely attracted. Before I left for

Paris in 1950, she came to New York, and we renewed our relationship. In 1957, she got a fellowship to Oxford and contacted me through the *International Herald Tribune*. She came to Paris for a visit and decided to stay there with me.]

DECEMBER 22

Susan is here—what a beauty she is! But I dislike so much about her . . . the way she sings, girlish and off key, the way she dances, rhythmless and fake sexy. I got annoyed with her for having an upset stomach at the Eiffel tower and also at the *cinémathèque* last night. Poor kid! I don't really think I'm attracted to her at all, but then, she says she loves me, and I need to hear that right now!

No word from Irene, and I keep thinking about Romaine; do I still love her?

Susan's vulnerability and insecurity displease me. She seems so naïve. Is she honest? I can't really believe she means what she says.

JANUARY 13, 1958

Irene, Irene . . . my real and only love. Last night in bed I called Susan "Pupi," my pet name for Irene and shocked myself. I started to cry, and Susan tried to comfort me by throwing her big body over me protectively. How heavy, how brusque she is!

I must write about my recent visit to Dublin, where my sister is living. I had sex there with an actor named Charlie Roberts, very charming and macho. He kept his socks on in bed. (It's awfully cold in Dublin this time of year.) Best sex I've had in a long time. My sister's lover, the theater director, Paddy, is an exciting man but so afraid of emotion; he won't be good for her in the end.

What shall I do about Susan? Just lie back and enjoy being loved? And my jealousy reflex is being activated big time, with everyone wanting her, men and women. Although I don't really care for her, I envy her success.

We are moving to my old hotel, the Poitou, probably a mistake—I don't like her smell. My sister says that's what's most important.

JANUARY 21

Blessed solitude! Susan has gone back to England for a week. I felt a bit lonely yesterday, but today I am enjoying being alone again. I'm back here in Irene's maids' room, which is mine now. Being at the Poitou with S was painful; the place so permeated with I's presence. But here in this room, I am happy recalling our crazy afternoons of sex, our remembering at the last minute, to turn off the light, pull the curtain. Our haste; our fast-coming mutual pleasure.

JANUARY 22

Peaceful time in my sun-filled tower. I might be getting my old translating job again. How swell that would be . . . freedom refound! The stove is not working . . . freezing!

JANUARY 23

Got a good fire going. The poor black wood-and-coal man just struggled up all these stairs with fifty kilos of wood on his back. We're not allowed to use the elevator. I always feel guilty when he comes; it seems so awful for him to have to do this. *Les riches salauds!*

Just got back from epilation. My dear Mlle. Christiane has disappeared again, so I went to a strange place in the neighborhood, a rather sordid joint. The woman who did my legs had long, straight hair hanging down from her armpits. She was wearing a low-cut sleeveless dress, in this weather! A sneaky-looking gray-haired man kept coming into the room to watch. Then, she took me to the shower to rinse off my poor, burning thighs. It was dark in the room, and I could hear a man and a woman talking quietly. Some day I must write a story about the perverse atmosphere of these beauty salons, where women repair their physical defects in secret, away from husbands and lovers.

FEBRUARY 5

I am working hard on the translation, a way to recover my freedom, at least from the [Trib.] job. But I am still caught in a dilemma, a choice between loneliness and Susan. I already dread the thought of our travel plans, being alone with her in places where I don't know anyone. I am sure I've never been in such an absurd situation, living with someone I neither desire sexually nor feel strongly about. At least with Sven, the sex was often good, and the security of being with a man in social environments was a definite advantage. It's very decadent, and I feel awful about it.

FEBRUARY 25

I have just a few more days at the Trib. Susan and I are living in a flat borrowed from Sam Wolfenstein. It's great being in an apartment, although it also means she never lets me out of her sight. What will happen when I'm no longer working at night? Will we be stuck together twenty-four hours a day? Our sexual relationship is really bad. When I do, infrequently, make love to her, I am either drunk and incompetent or technical, brutal, and cold. It's hideous of me, but what can I do? I'm simply not attracted to her. Even her tenderness repels me, her tentative touch . . . so unreal.

Today, I had made a date with a Negro man at the Flore, and he stood me up. Susan insisted on coming with me on the metro, saying she was going to the Deux Magots. I guess it serves me right that he didn't show, but I was really looking forward to getting laid!

All of this winter's lucky breaks—the translation, the apartment—seem to underline my real unhappiness. If only I weren't so afraid of being alone!

MARCH 15

My sister Bobbie is here! Our connection is strained, although some of our childhood closeness remains. She smuggled this notebook to me so S wouldn't see it . But she is such a flirt that it embarrasses me. She already has come on to Han. I'm beginning to think she wants to fuck all my old lovers. It's as if our childhood competition for Daddy's love is still going on. My feelings toward her range from harsh disapproval to a distant tenderness.

The bottom line, I think, is that I'm really fed up with women. Susan is more relaxed now but still so quick to take offense, so vulnerable. Those anxious eyes, probing my mood, remind me annoyingly of my mother!

At the flea market today, it was clear how totally I

dominate her. If I picked up some buttons, examined a doll, pointed out a necklace, she immediately enthused, "Oh, I like that! Oh, that's the prettiest!" Her desire to please me is embarrassing. I simply must do something about this relationship. It is hurtful to her and makes me feel guilty. What a coward I am! I should have simply ended it. But of course, when she leaves, I'll suffer my usual abandonment anxiety all over again.

MARCH 26, MY BIRTHDAY!

Susan is being very sweet, as usual. I got presents from Dad and Bobbie, but nothing from Irene, not even a word.

APRIL 3, HOLY WEEK
SEVILLA, SPAIN

We just got here, after two days in Madrid. I am sitting on the bed in the typically dim Spanish electric light. Susan is under the covers with her eyes closed. Music comes up through the open patio doors from the *fonda* downstairs. We've just been to watch a *Semana Santa* procession. The crowds are noisy and detached, as if they were at a show. I bet they take football games more seriously. But I found it tremendously moving. To add to the drama, a *saeta* (lament) rose up from across the square. Watching the *penitentes* in their pointed hoods, shapeless gowns, bare, bloody feet; some with chains on their ankles; some carrying heavy wooden crosses or gaudy, candle-lit figures of saints in velvet and gold, my eyes filled with helpless tears.

Susan drives me mad with her long scholarly explanations of things one only needs the eyes and ears of someone like Irene to see. At the Prado, she discoursed at length on Bosch and just now, explained that women are the backbone of the Church. I find these textbook dissertations of hers unbearable!

And of course, to make things more difficult, I can't stop thinking of Irene. This was inevitable given this language, these streets and *tapas* bars, and these beautiful, plump Spanish girls with their gorgeous round asses.

APRIL
TANGIERS, MOROCCO

This is by far the best part of the trip. The unwanted, sometimes hostile male attention we received in Sevilla is gone. As soon as we left there, and those awful men who groped and insulted us, things improved. Cadiz, surprisingly, was extremely beautiful and pleasant. The provincial Spanishness of Sevilla is there mitigated by a more cosmopolitan outlook. We stayed in a splendidly decaying hotel, the Loreto, in a room overlooking the green-blue sea. Walking along the seawall, gangs of children followed us, mostly laughing little boys, some really beautiful. One came after us and asked for money. I said, "Why should I give you anything? You've given me nothing . . . " He thought about that for a minute and then accepted it with a child's crystal-clear rationality. Of course, I called him back and gave him a coin.

Now, we are in fantastic Tangiers, a really international city. People speak many languages: Arabic, Spanish, French, Italian, and communicate quite well in all of them.

The Arab men are tall and handsome in their *djellabas,* and their behavior is dignified, not like the rug sellers on the Boul'Mich'.

Our room in the hotel, La Grande Poste, is big and fragrantly clean. It looks out over the port. The sea, a mating of Atlantic and Mediterranean, is calm and dark. In the morning, when we open the metal shutters, the light is dazzling. We had coffee in the tearoom at the sultan's palace, seated on cushions on the floor.

Last night we went to a bar, La Mar Chica, where a beat-up Spanish woman came on to both of us. A tiny creature, who looked like an old child, sang Flamenco badly.

Today we visited an American lesbian couple,

Sandy and Mary, who live here. Mary is an attractive gray-haired woman with a voluptuous body. Sandy is the typical, handsome, blonde college-girl type, California dyke. Their apartment was all cozy and modern, in mediocre taste. "What shall we give them to drink?" Sandy asks Mary. They play bridge weekly with "the girls." It's all very domestic and boring.

We leave Tangiers tomorrow. It's depressing with Susan, up and down, as always.

APRIL 30
PARIS

In the *jardins du Luxembourg*, a bright, warm day.

Oh, I wish Susan would go away; she bores and depresses me. Strangely, my sister is becoming a welcome presence. She is so alive now; so sexual; she inspires me. Irene is in New York, living her new life and forgetting me. I am forgetting her too. Not completely, but remembering is becoming optional. I'm not compelled to do it, as I was.

MAY 14

It's her birthday, and I haven't heard from her in weeks. In spite of what I wrote above, I haven't really forgotten her and am terribly dragged with Susan.

Yesterday, she said she was moving out. If only I had the strength to let her go instead of weakly saying, "I'd rather you didn't," which she eagerly seized upon as a plea for her to stay.

We're living in a charming place, the Hôtel Sainte Marie-Gallia. I love the dark wood floors and the *patronne* and the polite, gentle maids.

Last night, because I had told her it was Irene's birthday, Susan came to me in bed, and we made sweet love. But sadly, I just can't love her!

MAY 20
STRASBOURG

It's crisis time in France. The *République* is falling victim to its own weakness, pettiness, meanness, complacency. People are fleeing Paris. There is fear of a right-wing coup led by the *pieds noirs* (French colonists in Algeria). Last night, Sydney Leach nervously invited us to "come and sleep in the lab tonight if you want to see action"; little groups all over Paris are keeping vigils, preparing for a fight.

We hitchhiked out. I am glad not to be there tonight while my beloved, free, libertine city is under attack by the *salauds*, as Sartre calls them, the paratroops, the right-wingers, racists.

Just now, in the big, empty café on the square, we watched two paratroopers celebrating. They had bought a Paris paper, with a rude remark to the old paper seller, and banging their fists on the table, shouted, "*On les aura!*" (We'll get them).

We're on our way to Germany—to Munich (Nanna), Berlin, and Hamburg (Reinhard). Susan read yesterday's diary entry, and it's embarrassing to be writing in bed with her, but I am demonstrating my right to privacy!

JUNE 7, 1958
BERLIN

It is seven years since my first trip here, and the city has changed enormously. This afternoon, I lay on the grass in Tiergarten, now rich and fruitful, not like the wasteland it was in 1950. I'd been really cold to S the past three days, until sex this morning broke the deadlock. Why do I take my frustrations out on her? Part of it is jealousy; she gets so much attention. It's not her fault. But I pick on her annoying little mannerisms like, "As you know, VW's are very popular in the States," "As you know, of course . . . .blah, blah, blah." It's really mean of me to attack her awkward use of her hands when she speaks. I shouldn't be taking my helpless fury out on her!

JUNE 11, ON THE TRAIN TO HAMBURG

Just had my new passport stamped by the West German police. It has a rather impressive selection of
stamps in it already . . . we've traveled a lot this year.
We will see Reinhard in Hamburg, and it's sure to
be a disaster, given his wife, his crush on Susan,
and mine on him. A little old red-cheeked peasant
woman sits opposite us and sucks her teeth noisily.

JUNE 23
PARIS

Memories of Hamburg. On horseback in the hippo-
drome, Reinhardt behind me. I turn to him in the
saddle, and he smiles weakly. How beautiful he is!
On the beach, rolling his head in the sand. I had a
dream that night in which I held his head against my
breast, feeling its weight. On the beach, when I said,
"It's hot," he misheard and asked, "What's hard, Harriet?" And then that awful, drunk, conversation in
the bar when he said, "No, I can't love you . . . I have
my own life . . ."

On the whore street at night with S and R. Anxiety. Susan's terrible beauty eclipses me totally. I wish
she weren't my only source of love . . .

Back here a letter from Barbara Bank, saying,
"Irene has probably written you that I am coming to

Europe, etc. Feel very warm and good towards you."
Sure, now that Irene is no longer with me!

JULY 6

We leave for Greece on Wednesday, and I'm in a mad
rush to finish the translation, get money, pack, etc.
It's been a gray, rainy spring. I'm so busy, I have no
time for misery. In a month, Susan will leave for the
States and everything will change. I wanted to write
about our trip to Brittany with my sister, but I just
don't have the energy. Except for, oh yes, that early
morning on the beach at Saint-Michel-en-Greves, lying alone on the rocks as the sun rose, feeling strong!
And the wonderful little white room we had, with
the high bed and the window with steps up to it.
Dinner in the dining room, with its view of the pink
and blue sunset over the waves.

JULY 14
ATHENS

Just came in from the desert-like heat of the afternoon street to the cool darkness of our hotel room.
It's furnished very simply, no carpets, a big bed, a
small sink. . . . We are on Euripides Street (Evripidou), a market street full of trucks and vegetables.

An enormous trolley roars through it, shaking the buildings. We were told this hotel is also a brothel. We fit right in . . . no questions asked.

On Saturday night, we went with Takis, the sculptor from Paris, to the bouzouki bars to watch the working men dancing, alone and in couples, slowly and hypnotically . . . very erotic.

Yesterday we were at the Acropolis, with its soft, fleshy, pink marble. You can almost taste it. The blue sky gleams through the spaces in the roof. From there, you can see all the other hills that encircle the city. Off to the left is Piraeus and the sea, opaque silver, ridged like a leaf.

JULY 16

Late afternoon in the white room on Evripidou Street. I lie naked on the white bed. Out the window is the ruined roofscape, crumbling buildings with their innards exposed, a swatch of wallpaper, a corner of floor. The trolley car goes roaring by. Much talking and shouting in the street. The heat gets me very sexed-up, but there's nothing to do about it. At least when she's not here, I can enjoy my fantasies.

This morning, I walked across a field of stones, pillars, giants, seated women solid in the white heat of the Theseion. The Keramikos cemetery, with its singing locusts and sweet-smelling pines. In the small museum, there was a very alluring smiling sphinx with long pink curls and strong leonine haunches.

I am being awful to Susan as always. This morning when she asked me why I was "angry," I said, "I just can't stand seeing you twenty-four hours a day!" And she answered mildly, "It won't be much longer," which is true and made me feel even nastier.

I like the food here—rice pudding for breakfast, fish and salad for lunch in the workingmen's tavernas. Yesterday, I had a plate with one stuffed zucchini, one stuffed pepper, and one stuffed eggplant. Lovely, subtle differences between them.

I wonder . . . could I live here? I do like the men!

DELPHI

Sitting in the Tholos (a round building in Doric style, says our guide book). This is the sanctuary of Athena Pronaea, the almost flat remains of two temples. There is a deafening concert of cicadas, punctuated by the delicate tinkle of an ass's bell from higher up on the hill. Big green flies buzz angrily about. There are high mountains all around us, and way down, below the village, is a large, flat body of water, an inlet of the sea. The olive trees are old and enormous. Fragments of columns lie around like logs. We had lunch on the terrace at the cliff's edge: rice, to-

matoes, onions, black olives, clear, cold water. This
is heaven! An enormous eagle just flew right past us!

HYDRA

Now, another island in my life . . . I sit at the café on
the windy quay in bright sunshine.

Bobbing boats, thrumming motors, dark, bare-
footed people, white church steeple, white houses on
the hill. It could be Ibiza, but sadly, it is not.

Susan has gone to Athens to see about money.
Our landlord just rushed out shouting for two hundred drachmas. What a fright! He must have seen
Susan getting on the boat and thought we were cut-
ting out on our bill.

I just shook my head, "yes," for grapes, forgetting
that that means "no" here, so the waiter took them
away. He just brought them back, thanks.

I stretched dinner out as long as I could. Now I'm
at a café, sitting not too close to the foreign in-crowd.
I don't intend to be depressed. In fact, I feel better
than I usually do when S is here. She has a way of
making me feel isolated, alone with her. God knows,
though, this group is repulsive . . .

Susan will leave soon. I suppose I will miss her,
maybe more than I did Irene, since we were already
estranged before she left. Susan truly surrounds me
with affection. It's awful that I can't enjoy it and am

forever rejecting and criticizing. I guess I should be grateful for these nine months. I often feel a certain tenderness toward her. I did today when she left. She really is such a child, and though she can be annoying, her warmth is a child's, her sulking, too.

AUGUST 12
ATHENS

It's our last night here. Evripidou Street is quiet, except for the occasional rumble of the trolley. We just made our farewell appearance at Zonar's café, where a little, middle-aged lawyer said, sadly, "Oh, then we won't have the pleasure of seeing you again?" We seem to have been the dream girls of a small group of elderly men who have been watching our comings and goings.

Barbara Bank is here and gave me a tiny bouquet of wonderful, white, perfumed jasmine. She insists on talking about Irene, causing me much anguish. Susan took it well, after a small initial protest. Barbara kissed me, stroking my face, promising to write me in Paris. "Judas kiss," said Susan, wisely.

The worst part of it was her insistence on giving me details: "She had a fight with Adele," "She took me to a new girls' bar . . . "

Finally, Athens has been lovely. Such beauties in the museums: the marvelous archaic goddesses, the pale blue stone beads, a bird-shaped vase with its graceful throat bent back in abandon, a delicate gold Cycladic pin topped with a tiny ram's head.

AUGUST 26
PARIS

Susan left three days ago, and miraculously, I am suddenly surrounded by men! The Negro on Saturday, the painter on Sunday, and this big, handsome, perverse Henri, whose looks kill me! He is like a dark version of the actor Peter van Eyck, complete with a scar on his upper lip.

AUGUST 27

Letter from Susan. Her first days in New York have been painful. I got a certain nasty satisfaction from that. Had a note from Sven inviting me to come to Lacoste whenever I want. Dinner at Gregory Corso's. A German girl there kept looking at me, murmuring "Renaissance" and stroking my hair. She seemed upset by the silly argument I was having with Corso which, actually, I was only pursuing to get her attention.

August 31

Slept with Henri last night. He's an admirer of the Marquis de Sade. His big body is horribly scarred and covered with thick black hair. He has a strange, unpleasant odor and sweats a lot. My sister says that's a sign of fear. He kept ramming me with that enormous prick, but neither of us ever came. I was too conscious and maybe a little afraid of him. As always, *all the effort in the world cannot call Eros from heaven!*

Tonight, I can't stop thinking of Irene. Susan is out of sight, out of mind. But last night, at the Trois Fontaines with Henri, I put "Love is Strange" (our song) on the jukebox and it never came on. I felt superstitious about that . . . trying and failing to exorcise her.

I don't really want to go to Lacoste.

September 4

I slept with Henri again last night, in my room. Sex was better, but not great. He says it will be soon. After he left, I couldn't sleep, worrying about my feelings for him. I'm sure there's nothing he despises more than a woman in love with him.

I woke up around eight with an awful pain in my abdomen and went into the hall to the john. A voice in my head kept saying, "Take the key," but I ignored it, and sure enough, my door slammed shut as I entered the WC. What could I do? I was on the verge of hysterics with that pain in my gut, when, miraculously, there was a sweet-faced young girl in a blue nurse's uniform, standing in front of my room saying, "My key fits." And she unlocked my door with a warm smile. If she hadn't been there, I think I would have lain down on the cold tile floor and howled like a dog.

Turns out, the pain was from my period, which just got blood all over the sheets. My box is so sore the Tampax hurt going in. Luckily, I have the kif and whiskey Henri brought to ease the pain.

SEPTEMBER 7

Slept all day; it's now five in the afternoon. I had a dream about reconciling with Alfred. I remember saying, "You know why we can't be friends," and looking at Arthur, his lover.

Corso screaming the other night: "I'm too beautiful for you and your lousy friends!" It's a cry I've often felt in myself but was too proud to utter. I feel very close to Gregory in a strange, neurotic way.

I am on the quay, looking at an edition of Verlaine's *Parallèlement* which Henri told me about. The old lady *bouquiniste*, the owner of the stand, rushed over to me saying, "*Verlaine, c'est vraiment intéressant, Mlle.*" She obviously thought I was a lesbian, since the poems are all about that. I really don't understand why Baudelaire and company were so fascinated by them. Can you imagine a woman writing a book about homosexual men?

Bobbie has taken a job at the Lido nightclub as a *mannequin*, which is what they call the tall beauties who stand around in extravagant topless costumes while the British Bluebells, the dancers, do their jobs. I am fascinated by the scene, and sometimes join her and the girls after the club has closed when they go out on the town to relax. Last night, I went with Bobbie and two dancers, Shirley and Pamela, to a bar they like called Le Calvados. They are very sexy-looking girls but actually rather prim. I got very drunk and sang "I've Got It Bad" with the black piano player. Sounded great, they tell me.

I'm thinking about Susan . . . I really didn't love her and still don't. It's sort of satisfying to recognize that I don't just automatically fall in love with anyone who wants me . . . that there is some truth to my feelings.

Looking through these pages, I read last September's entries. That was the nightmarish visit to Alfred when I was desperately depressed.

SEPTEMBER 17

No word from Henri. It was obvious he had lost interest by our second night in bed. His tone had changed
completely, and he forgot to borrow the books he had
so eagerly asked for.

Well, then there's this American, Baird, a sad fellow too much into drugs. He needs guidance and
gentleness, not my thing. Though it was fun dancing
with him Saturday night. We danced together surprisingly well. I said, "You dance just like I do," and
he replied, "Yeah, man; that's it, man, etc." And then,
"Wow, I'm sure glad I talked to you. For five years
now I've been thinking you must be the swingin-
gest chick!" But he just sat around, waiting for me to
make a move and then got angry and said, "I'm tired
of waiting!" and we went our separate ways.

My sister is back with her boyfriend and is more
independent now. Last spring, when she was around
a lot, Susan wrote in her journal (I sneaked a peek)
that she resented B's constant presence.

Susan writes less often, a sign she is starting to
enjoy her New York life. I am glad; I was getting fed
up with one letter a day, once even two!

The other night at the Tournon, drinking gaily
with Bill, the black American writer, and Han and
Monique, we ended up going to their house. I expected, not too enthusiastically, that I would sleep
with Bill, but it turned out he wanted Monique. So

Han said, "Let's fly away somewhere," and we went to the other room. "I love you, you know," he said, but the fuck was no good at all and he kept repeating "I like to fuck you," over and over, obviously trying to convince himself.

This morning, as I lay in bed with gray Paris light filtering through the window blind, street noises, a canary singing somewhere, I imagined I was in New York, and it was exciting. Think about it . . .

SEPTEMBER 19
LACOSTE

The night before I left Paris, I went to an orgy with Henri. Most of the time, he was busy with other people, coming around every once in a while to check on me. Once or twice, he tried something, but I pushed him away in favor of some skinny, hairless old man or other. Why? To show my independence, perhaps . . .

The first thing I saw on entering was a pot-bellied man with a big erection being blown by a kneeling, flabby, droopy-breasted woman. Other pink, hairy shapes stood in shadow all around. I was immediately shocked and had an urge to laugh hysterically, what the French call *le fou-rire*. A distinguished-looking old gentleman stroked my ass in the corner, welcoming me, the newcomer. Then Henri called me from the other room to come and watch some frowsy female blowing another one. I finally got into the act after diddling around with an ugly, impotent man on a bed. Henri presented me to a dyke who very inexpertly caressed me, not letting me touch her. Then I went down on a pretty girl, who came all over the place and made a big fuss about how wonderful I was. And so I became the *vedette* (star) of the party. Three or four people were doing various things to me, including one monstrous woman going down on me clumsily. At last, I was rescued by the arrival of the one attractive man there, a Russian, who fucked me very well and brought me to a real orgasm, which drove all that false sex play out of my head.

Then Henri was caressing me while another man watched, getting excited. Henri has a hard time getting it up but enjoyed "preparing" me for someone else to fuck. And on and on, in various scenarios without much joy in them.

I finally went down on the skinny impotent man, who at last managed to produce a few bitter drops from his little prick.

I learned a few things from this experience. A great fuck can join two strangers in something that resembles love. Most people are sexless. I still feel good with women, affectionate, familiar.

Afterward, we went to a jazz club and danced. How sad that, while dancing tightly entwined, after an orgy for God's sake, he managed to say, "*Tu me fais presque bander quand tu danse comme ça."* (You *almost* get me hard when you dance like that). How sad!

Now I am in Lacoste. We went to a bullfight yesterday in Arles . . . pure pleasure! Watching Chamaco, the beautiful gypsy, almost made me come . . .

SEPTEMBER 21

Sven is finally releasing his anger. Romaine remains distant. He is into the mean heart of the matter, and has managed to eliminate any vestigial tenderness he may have felt for me. In truth, whatever affection I still had for him is now dissolved into a pure fluid of contempt. I don't hate him, but I despise his hypocritical, leftist holier-than-thou, puritanical self-righteousness. He's a failure at everything, even farming! Meanwhile, Romaine just floats around, noncommittal and seductive.

SEPTEMBER 29

Just back from Saint-Tropez. The sea, the nude beaches, dancing in the bars at night; it was great, exactly what I needed to recover from the dark atmosphere at Lacoste.

They are living a really dreary life there. Except for their art, it's a daily routine of uninteresting tasks, bad food, prim politics, pleasureless flirtations.

One night, I wanted Romaine and couldn't get to sleep, thinking she would come to me. I said, "*J'attendais*," but no one was there. I peered into the darkness and thought it was Sven. I said, "Sven?" but there was no answer, and I panicked and finally realized I was dreaming.

I'm a bit anxious about the possibility of being pregnant. If I were, I wouldn't know by whom.

I am glad of Susan's regular letters. Without them I'd start forgetting who I am.

OCTOBER 16
PARIS

This letter she gave me. Why had she saved it? She, who is so afraid of being discovered by Sven. I read it in the blast of the mistral and didn't understand it. Now I've read it again, here in my quiet room, and it has made me weep. After all those awful nights, when I waited, silent in the dark, hoping to hear her stealing toward me, we had finally reached each other, when Sven stormed into the attic room at Evelyne's and flung himself at us on the bed. I was afraid and ran out, leaving her to him. I could hear him hitting her while she held back her cries so our hostess, downstairs, wouldn't be awakened. I stayed quiet in the next room, straining my ears to hear them, to learn if she would deny me.

Just before he raged in, I had said, "*Promets-moi que tu resteras avec moi toute la nuit,*" and she had answered yes and hugged me tighter. And then he burst in, screaming, bullying, threatening to kill himself.

Yesterday, at the café in Apt, I was cruel and cold, accusing her of deception. At night, Sven took my bags to the truck. She disappeared as we drove off, and I called out into the night, "*Romaine, Romaine, viens dire au revoir!*" Of course, she didn't come, but I knew she heard me, my poor, demonic, unbalanced love.

From her letter: "*Tu ne sais pas combien de fois j'ai pleuree sur toi,*" "*Je t'aime, plus que ton Irene t'aimait,*" "*Je suis malade chaque fois que tu pars.*" And in that narrow bed, before Sven crashed in, "*C'est comme à Paris les premières fois, rue Jouvenet; tu te souviens?*" (It's like Paris, the first time, rue Jouvenet; do you remember?") Of course I do, my love.

OCTOBER 16

Soon begins the hardest journey, the journey home. . . . After all these years, I am starving in my beloved Paris. Why is it so empty. Why am I so alone?

SATURDAY NIGHT . . . SUNDAY MORNING

And suddenly, not really alone. A letter from Romaine waits for me under the door on my return from an amusing but pointless Tournon evening with Iris, Han, and Monique.

OCTOBER 26

I'm certainly going to sound paranoid, but this is absolutely true. Someone has drilled a hole in my thin wooden door; someone who wants to watch me, I suppose. Could it be the young blond man I saw coming from the servants' entrance yesterday, as I was going in? After I passed him, he stopped dead in the courtyard and watched me until I headed up the stairs.

I plugged the hole with candle wax, but now it looks as if someone had tried to poke through it. So I've tacked a postcard over it, a Ravenna mosaic of Christ Redeemer. Surely that will protect me.

Just got back from Hanna's, where we talked of S and R; of loneliness, rejection, lost friends. Her American husband, Reggie, recently left her, and she seems totally devastated. I told her I feel my life in Paris has been a failure. She was very kind and replied, "That's ridiculous; you're young and good-looking and you have your writing!" She also told me that Sven had suffered terribly when I broke up with him, which surprised me. I had thought he was already with Romaine.

OCTOBER 29

I have been having this scary and vaguely exciting feeling of being watched; of hearing suspicious sounds from the hall. But I've blocked the hole in the door and can't find another. Guess I'm just hard up; the old maid looking under the bed.

No news from Susan. It makes me nervous, since I will be moving in with her soon in New York.

OCTOBER 30

I look into the sweet brown eyes of my Evzone doll . . . pleasant memories. Susan is going through hell with her divorce. Sort of like my situation with my mother, tied to a "dying animal"—in her case, the marriage.

My stove works well, burning all day. I am only content here, in this little attic, with its skylight looking out over rain-shiny Paris roofs.

NOVEMBER 9

I am alone but not unhappy; far less than last year when I dragged myself along with Susan, frustrated and annoyed. Now I am all in one piece; my solitude is my own, not shared with someone who troubles me. And I have absolutely no interest in women! Slept with Han again the other night; not great but I really needed it. Han tells me he and his wife have "an understanding." And then he went on, "But *you* don't understand me . . . " Duh!

Went to the Trois Fontaines last night and was bored stiff. I guess I am just not queer anymore. Couldn't even get interested in Isabelle, an attractive girl who has eyes for me.

NOVEMBER 18

Slept with Nick Arnold; another failure. We've been drawn to each other for years at a distance, but it's too late now, a too-delayed climax. We were in my room, drunk, at ten in the morning; the bed too small; we too nervous and self-conscious. He is beautiful and intelligent but so neurotic! What a shame . . . he has destroyed my tranquility. But at least I really know what I want now; a man, a man I could live with!

I'm terribly bugged by Bobbie. Nanna once asked, "Didn't she take all your boyfriends away from you?"

It's true that she always interferes whenever I seem interested in someone. She can't help being such a sexy number, but I cringe when she starts flirting, those cute smiles, that phony, naïve manner. I guess this is just jealousy, the old "sibling rivalry." But what really bugs me is that, after all these years in Paris, I am about to be known as "Barbara's sister!"

NOVEMBER 23

Nick again. Another long, ill-fated night. We went to the Mars Club to hear Billie Holliday. Her voice is tired and cracked but still full of passion. Nick didn't get it at all, kept struggling to say what he really means, doesn't want to be influenced by "beer and music." Then went to Bantu to dance, but it wasn't like the first time. He, hot and breathless; I cool. A week ago, I was totally turned on to him. This time, I didn't feel sex, probably because of how lousy it was then. In the dreary morning light we sat at the Escurial, on my corner, and I tried to eat a pâté sandwich that made me nauseous. No, he wasn't coming upstairs with me: "What for? It won't do either of us any good!"

Okay.

He kisses me goodbye in the hall. "I'd like to mix my life up with yours, Harriet, but I can't!" he whines.

"Come upstairs, honey." I am too tired to argue but can't really believe he won't.

"I can't!"

"Okay, so long," and up the weary stairs I go, listening for his footsteps, following or leaving, but neither; he doesn't move.

I went to sleep in my small, lonely bed; had bad dreams and woke up at two in the afternoon hearing voices in the hall. "*Savez-vous, Monsieur, ou habite Mlle. Sohmers?*"

And here's Nick, all cleaned up, shaved, fresh and shiny, carrying a big bunch of red, white, and pink carnations!

I wash my swollen face and get back into bed. And then it all falls apart. I am so ready, but he can't seem to find me. Then he finally gets in and I'm almost coming . . . oh sweet . . . and then BANG! He's done; premature ejaculation maximus! He's frantic. He howls, "Oh God, I think about you, and I think I know how it will be, but it just doesn't work!" We lie in bed for hours; he smokes one cigarette after another; talking, talking. . . . Night fills the skylight. I want to go to the *bains-douches* and take a shower.

We finally get up.

"I won't come again," he says. And, at the bottom of the stairs, "I probably won't come again; my girlfriend will be back soon and anyway . . . Sorry . . . "

Goodbye, love. I am in pain. He is beautiful, but he has all these hangups about American women and intellectuals. I am a wreck . . . too much alcohol, too many splintered expectations. I suddenly feel sure that I can't go back to Susan!

NOVEMBER 21

Saw a Bergman movie, *Rêve de femmes*. Afterward I went out into the rainy street, had a horrible sandwich and milkshake at SIP Babylone, and then went down to the Monaco, where I met Han and Monique. She has the idea that Han should make me pregnant. She keeps bringing it up, and he agrees. They don't know it, but a few years ago I had the same thought, though now I have my doubts. Besides, I've never been pregnant; probably barren.

Monique says, "*Tu ne dois pas retourner vivre avec Susan, non, non. Alors, reste ici! Ne rentre pas à New York!*"

NOVEMBER 26

The little painter, Stasha, said last night, "I heard so much about your sister, but you are more beautiful than she . . . " I was flattered, but appalled that people now know me as "Barbara's sister" when it should be the other way around.

Last night I had sex with Victor Pinto in an anonymous apartment somewhere in Passy. Erroll Garner and the MJQ were on the phonograph, and we had a great time! His small, skinny body is attached to a big, bristling, but temperamental cock. For some reason, I just couldn't come, maybe because it was so emotionless. I am not the way I used to be; just come whenever. I seem to want something more: words, gestures, meaning . . . But he is sweet and good in bed. Afterward we ate canned corn and chicken soup and peaches. And later we drove through dark, empty streets that could have been in New York, and I wished they were and that we were heading for some Village bar to dance and get drunk.

The rest of the night was awful. I had that horrible business, like last month, murderous cramps and nausea for hours. I even threw up. It's as though my body doesn't want to give up that precious egg for another childless month.

December 8

Made it with Victor again. Good as he is, I can't come with him. I guess the chemistry just isn't there. I still think about Nick. Spent the evening at the Tournon; so dreary, incestuous, gossipy, like a nagging family.

Had an awkward letter from Sven. Does he really want me to come to Lacoste? And should I?

DECEMBER 12

The fourth anniversary of my mother's death, and I've lit a candle in her memory. It is lovely, flickering yellow in its little glass. I've set it in front of an old photo of her where she looks pretty, my lovely, ugly mother . . .

Last night I had another sad session with Nick. He got my note about the room and came in a hurry. Said he couldn't sleep. Had gone out looking for me at the Select and then the Tournon, where I had stayed late. What a shock when I saw him and had my old happy reaction.

It's always the same. First, I'm wild with hope, but then things go sour. He walked away without a kiss goodbye at my door. I ran after him. He seemed to have gone a great distance. I caught him by the arm like a beggar. Long, dreary talk at the café, and out in the morning, at 9:30, he said, smiling coolly, "Well, you don't want me to kiss you goodbye?"

"No."

"Adios, then," and we turned away from each other.

I slept three hours, until noon. My failure with Nick has made one thing very clear; I don't desire women any more!

DECEMBER 14

I am having a hard time being accepted as a woman. After all these years, my reputation works against me. I am still seen as a lesbian, and some men like that image. I am sure Victor does and maybe even Nick. But I don't want it anymore. Tonight I behaved very femininely when I refused to go home with Victor. I am tired of this game.

JANUARY 3, 1959
PARIS

Drove up from Lacoste yesterday through mountains, snow, rain, night . . . dinner and a drink. It was all beautiful! Here, letters are waiting from Susan and others. New York sounds awful. Truly, I think there is more for me here than there. How I dislike those American faces in the mail room at Amex! Strangely, my sister phoned this morning and said she hates Paris and is thinking of going home. If she did, would that make things better for me here?

I want to write about Lacoste and how different it was this time, but I can't seem to think straight. I'm full of anxiety and keep hoping for a miracle that will keep me here, something to tip the scales, as Irene once said.

JANUARY 11

Wild night, high, drunk. Danced with a tall German boy at Herta's party. Marie-Pierre came on to me; Louis Armstrong and Ella. It was the same record I heard at Pfriem's in Lacoste, when Maxime de la Falaise and I had that flirtatious conversation that went on too long. "You show me yours . . . etc.," exciting but unpleasant too.

There was a German painter there who had lost an arm. The first thing he said to me when we danced was, "You know I have only one arm." That's his claim to fame apparently.

But later, in the hotel room, he acted shocked when I tried to suck on the stump! I had gone with him after the tall, handsome German with the big erection walked out on me. Herta said he always does that.

So the one-armed guy and I went to Les Halles and roamed around. It started to snow, and we stopped in front of Samaritaine, the department store, and looked in the windows. An old man came over and said, "*C'est fermé*," as if dumb foreigners like us had to be told that.

We walked across the Pont Neuf and down rue Dauphine, got to the Monaco at eight a.m., and played the pinball machine. He said a lot of crazy things: his first night in Paris; he wanted to go mad. Finally, we went to his hotel and had frantic, violent, unsuccessful sex. I was nuts and said things like, "I love cripples," which is totally untrue.

By some miracle, I woke up at 2:20 p.m. and made it to my appointment with Sydney and Bobbie to drive out to the country. It was lovely, rows and rows of tall snowy trees. We ate at the Château de Guermantes (!) in a little inn; the best steak I've had in years.

Bobbie says she's coming to New York with me. I feel very ambivalent about that.

JANUARY 12

I'm suddenly scared—afraid of potential situations in New York, which could develop from my lack of love for Susan and my leftover passion for Irene. And my little sister too in the mix. And an office job? How dreadful. At least here I'm not a clerk!

JANUARY 30, 1959

These crazy last days! Paris gives herself to me with sunshine. Mad things happen, like being on my bike and seeing Nick go into Pam Pam, and speeding happily on to American Express. Went to the john and then to the mail room, and there he was, poor thing, looking awful, pasty-faced, and glum. He lit up like a pinball machine when he saw me. "When are you leaving?" "When are you coming back?" "I thought you were already gone." "If you ever want to write me, you can use Amex."

"Why," said I bitchily, "would I want to write you?"

"Well, if you need anything done here, I'd be glad to do it."

"Thank you!" I said and rode off in a hurry to later appointments.

Tonight, *chez* Victor. We finally made it very well. Obviously taking pictures excites him, and me too. Also, he has a very talented tongue. I haven't come in so long, it really flipped me out! We fucked too, but he does have problems that way. Looking at me afterward, my awakened skin and body, Victor said, "Well, I've primed you for somebody else."

I have lists of things to do, mad with excitement, smelling trouble ahead. But whatever happens in New York, I must stay with men . . . that is what I really want!

FEBRUARY 8, 1959
ABOARD THE *QUEEN ELIZABETH*, SAILING HOME

. . .

Afterword

These pages from the years 1950 to 1959 are a record of the voyages, love affairs, friendships, disappointments, sorrows, and joys of my life abroad as a young adventurer experimenting with danger and passion.

As I feared and foresaw toward the end of my diaries, Susan and Irene did connect in New York, shattering my foolish self-confidence and purging forever any interest I had in women as lovers.

I moved on into relationships with men, teaching, writing, marriage, and motherhood.

Now, I am in my eighties. I read these pages with fascination, surprise, and a certain nostalgia, overjoyed by the realization that, in them, there is nothing to regret . . .

Spring 2014
Harriet Sohmers Zwerling

SPUYTEN DUYVIL

Meeting Eyes Bindery
Triton
Lithic Scatter

Made in United States
Orlando, FL
23 August 2023

36372500R00188